MAXIMIZE
YOUR RETIREMENT
INCOME

A Guide to Financial Decision
Making at Retirement

Scott M. Peterson, ChFC

Maximize Your Retirement Income: A Guide to Financial Decision Making at Retirement

Printed by Brigham Young University Print Services
Provo, Utah 84602

Peterson, Scott M., 1962-
    Maximize your retirement income : a guide to
financial decision making at retirement / Scott M.
Peterson.
    p. cm.
    Includes bibliographical references.
    LCCN 2010927984
    ISBN-13: 9780984387984
    ISBN-10: 0984387986

    1. Retirement--Planning. 2. Finance, Personal.
I. Title.

HQ1062.P48 2011   646.7'9
                    QBI11-600045

10 9 8 7 6 5 4 3 2 1

I dedicate this book to my best friend and companion Tracie and our five wonderful children, who remind me every day that the most precious things in this life really don't have anything to do with money.

ACKNOWLEDGEMENTS

This book originated during the market crash of 2008–9. I would truly be ungrateful if I did not acknowledge my loyal and experienced staff that, during this extraordinary era of market volatility, both assisted me in taking care of our existing clients and aided me in generating ideas for the book.

Thanks to Cindy Camphuysen for the dependable, efficient, and friendly way she serves our clients. Then, to Rachel Benner, whose attention to detail in helping me to manage portfolios and client accounts is ever appreciated. A special thanks to Sara Harris, who was hired as a marketing manager, but adapted to become a talented researcher, editor, and indispensible partner in getting this book published. Sara's exceptional writing abilities, attention to detail, and fearless ability to tell the boss when he's wrong added a lot to the book.

TABLE OF
CONTENTS

Introduction   **xi**

**Chapter 1: Opportunities and Risks Facing
Baby Boomers**   **1**
   Opportunity   2
   Risk   3

Chapter 2: The Retirement Income Plan   **11**
   What Is a Retirement Income Plan?   11
   What Is a Retirement Income Planner?   13
   The Accumulator vs. the Distributor   14
   Identifying Expenses   15
   Identifying and Maximizing All Sources of Income   16
   How Do I Put Together a Plan?   18

Chapter 3: The History and Future of Social Security   **21**
   Early American Methods of Financial Security   22
   The History of Social Security   23
   What Is Social Security?   25

How Important Is Social Security to Retirees Today?   26
Will Social Security Be There for Me?   27

Chapter 4: The Ins and Outs of Social Security   29
When Should I File?   30
How Benefits Are Calculated   31
Spousal Planning   34
Survivorship Planning   37
Divorced Spouse Benefits   40
Working While Receiving Benefits   41
Social Security Taxation   42
A Note about Medicare   43
Summary   44

Chapter 5: The Vanishing Pension   47
The Defined Benefit Pension Plan   48
The New Pension   49
The Pension Distribution Plan   50
The Pension Rollover   50
The Pension Dilemma   52
Know Your Pension Plan   58
Pension Guarantees   59
Conclusion   60

Chapter 6: Working during Retirement   61
Reasons for Working Longer   62
Calculating the Financial Impact of Working
During Retirement   65
How Much Longer Should I Work?   67
Old Careers vs. New Careers   68
Warning: Working During Retirement isn't
Always Possible   71
A Concluding Note   71

Chapter 7: Reverse Mortgages   **73**
Eligibility   75
Advantages of Reverse Mortgages   75
Disadvantages of Reverse Mortgages   79
The Application Process   80
Is a Reverse Mortgage a Good Option for You?   82

Chapter 8: Managing Investments during Retirement   **83**
Creating the Investment Management Plan   84
Investor Beware   93

Chapter 9: Annuities   **97**
Annuity Types and Guarantees   98
Death Benefit Guarantee   100
Guaranteed Minimum Withdrawal Benefits (GMWBs)   102
Disadvantages of Variable Annuities   108
A Concluding Note   111

Chapter 10: Withdrawal Strategies   **113**
Withdrawal Rates   114
Withdrawal Methodology   116
The Interest-Only Strategy   117
The "Annuitize Everything" Strategy   118
Systematic Withdrawal from a Balanced Portfolio   118
The Time-Segmented Distribution Strategy   121

Chapter 11: Putting It All Together   **125**
Situation One: Ben and Darla   126
Situation Two: Bruce and Katherine   128
Situation Three: Jerry and Ann   130
Conclusion   132

Chapter 12: Choosing the Right Advisor   **133**
What Does an Investment Advisor Actually Do?   134

How Do Retirement Income Planners Get Paid? 135
The Qualified Retirement Income Planner 137
How to Find a Retirement Income Planner 137
Regulation of Investment Professionals 138
Questions to Ask the Potential Investment Advisor 139

Conclusion **145**
Additional Resources **147**
Peterson Financial Website 147
Peterson Financial Income for Life® Website and Movie 147
Budgeting Web Sites 147
Pension Benefit Guaranty Corporation 148
Full-Time RVing 148
Background Checks on Financial Advisors 148
Social Security Online 148

Glossary **149**
Bibliography **159**

INTRODUCTION

This book is not about how to prepare for retirement; there are already thousands of books that have been written about that subject. Instead, this book will address the many financial decisions and considerations that retirees will need to make upon deciding to retire. These decisions vary widely, and include how to maximize Social Security benefits, how to invest properly during retirement, and how to distribute retirement funds so they last a lifetime. Decisions made at this time of life can make the difference between a financially successful retirement and failure. The intent of this book is not to provide all the answers about financial decision making at retirement, but rather to make retirees aware of the possibilities that should be discussed in greater detail with qualified financial, tax, and legal professionals.[1]

---

1. This material is for general information purposes only and should not be construed as specific investment advice. As with any investment strategies there are risks. Implementing any strategies mentioned does not guarantee against loss.

Since the beginning of my career in 1986, I have made a conscious effort to focus on and specialize in issues regarding retirement. My company, Peterson Financial and Retirement Services, has worked with and managed money for literally hundreds of retirees and their families. The sixty-five-year-old I started advising twenty-five years ago isn't sixty-five anymore. Thus I have seen firsthand what works, as well as what doesn't work, for retirees and their heirs during the various stages of the retirement process.

During my quarter of a century of managing money for retirees, I have experienced and seen an abundance of situations that may be helpful to you. It is my hope that the experiences related in this book, and my conclusions from years of academic research, will help future retirees arm themselves with enough basic knowledge to understand the issues associated with retirement distribution planning. With this information, hopefully retirees will be able to figure out how to financially maximize their respective retirement experiences.[2]

---

2. The case studies found in this book are based on real people and experiences, but all names and exact situations have been altered to maintain confidentiality.

CHAPTER 1

OPPORTUNITIES AND RISKS
FACING BABY BOOMERS

Whoa! What happened? you think, as you look into the mirror. Not too long ago, that same person staring back at you had many years to plan and prepare for retirement, but somewhere along life's highway, sometime during a child's soccer game, during staff meetings, during a hectic commute, time has passed you by. Now you've come to look like your parents, and you're really considering the possibility of retiring.

If this experience sounds familiar, you are in excellent company. Prominent politicians such as Bill Clinton, George W. Bush, and even the youthful Mitt Romney are among the first wave of baby boomers now becoming eligible for their Social Security checks. Notable entertainers and athletes reaching that milestone include Dolly Parton, Jimmy Buffet, Steven Spielberg, Kareem Abdul-Jabbar, Nolan Ryan, and Reggie Jackson.

Baby boomers, or people born between 1946 and 1964, are just starting to retire. The first wave came in 2008, when 3.2 million individuals retired. At the beginning of this baby boomer retirement era, 365 individuals will retire each hour. Eventually, ten thousand individuals will retire daily for the next twenty years, until the number of retirees hits roughly eighty million by the year 2030.

Financially speaking, some are better prepared than others for this significant, and sometimes frightening, change of life. Some have large 401(k)s, IRAs, stock options, and company-sponsored retirement plans, while others lack these luxuries. Some are debt-free and have large real estate holdings; others don't. Some have dreams of extensive travel and vacation homes, while some just dream of staying home. Some will be selling businesses or even working during their retirement years, while others will pursue hobbies and other interests. The point is that this next stage of life will be as individual as its eighty million participants. Everyone has dreamed of retirement, and most have prepared to a greater or lesser degree for this dramatic change of lifestyle, but few know how to manage their finances during this time.

Wherever the retirees-to-be find themselves along the financial retirement preparedness continuum, they will all be making decisions at retirement that will have a huge and lasting impact on their financial security for the remainder of what could be a very lengthy period of time. Most of these decisions are irreversible and should be made with the help of a qualified professional who can guide retirees through the process.

Even though individual retirement situations will be unique, all retirees have some things in common. For example, unlimited opportunities, as well as unprecedented risks, will be part of every retiree's future. And for most, properly managing assets during the retirement years to come will be challenging, as individuals will be personally responsible for working out a stream of income from their investments that may have to last as long as three decades.

Opportunity

Baby boomers' retirements will be very different from those of their parents and grandparents. Previous generations of retirees usually worked for the same company for most of their careers.

When they reached retirement age, they were given a gold watch and a monthly pension check, and they began a quiet retirement at home with their spouse. Life expectancies were shorter than those of people retiring today because of limited medical technology. The retirees of the past would usually spend a few years relaxing with family and friends before declining health made retirement short and unpleasant.

In contrast, there has never been a group of retirees as healthy, wealthy, educated, and active as the baby boomer retirees. Because of these factors, they can travel, develop new hobbies, and accomplish life goals. Some will choose to continue working; others will start a new career or business, go back to school, or simply relax and enjoy their "golden years" with friends and family. Whatever their individual choices, baby boomers have unprecedented opportunities at their disposal.

Risk

Despite the many opportunities available, several risk factors can derail a successful retirement. The foremost risks include:

- Longevity, or the risk of living too long
- Inflation
- Investment management risk

Since there is no way that individuals can realistically stop the problems of longevity and inflation, those topics will not be a focus of this book. However, having an understanding of the problems they present is essential. The third important risk factor, that of personal investment management, is a risk about which you can and need to be proactive. You can only combat the effects of longevity and inflation by implementing proper investment strategies. Different ways to combat risks associated with investment management will be discussed throughout this book.

Longevity

Scientific and medical advances over the past century have dramatically increased life expectancies. More infants now survive into adulthood, and more adults live into their eighties and nineties. This has changed the face of retirement planning. Previously, most retirees could expect to live five, ten, or fifteen years after retiring. Today, it's not uncommon to have twenty-, thirty-, or even forty-year retirements. At Peterson Financial, we currently manage money for a man who is actually 108 years old. He's not the norm, but his experience illustrates the importance of preparing for a long life.

Because of longer life expectancies, many retirees face the very real risk that they will outlive their money if they don't plan for a lengthy retirement. Simply stated, it's best to plan on living longer than even the current life expectancies estimate, because those estimates represent the average. To be certain, some people will die before life expectancy, but some will live beyond it—sometimes many years beyond it. Many people underestimate the amount of time they need to plan to be retired. A man age sixty-five has a 50 percent chance of living until age eighty-five, and a 30 percent chance of living to age ninety. These odds rise significantly for females; a woman who age sixty-five has a 62 percent chance of living until age eighty-five and a nearly 41 percent chance of living to age ninety[1] (see fig. 1.1).

---

1. Society of Actuaries, *RP-2000 Mortality Tables*, 2000, http://www.soa.org/files /pdf/rp00_mortalitytables.pdf.

	Life Expectancy at Age 65		
TO AGE:	SINGLE MALE	SINGLE FEMALE	AT LEAST ONE MEMBER OF A COUPLE
70	93.3%	95.8%	99.7%
75	82.8%	89.3%	98.2%
80	68.0%	78.6%	93.1%
85	49.3%	62.2%	80.8%
90	29.5%	40.6%	58.1%
95	13.4%	19.4%	30.2%

fig. 1.1
Source: Society of Actuaries 2000 U.S. Annuity Table

Due to the high odds that their life spans will be long, it is vital that preretirees and retirees plan their investment strategies to provide income for a lifetime rather than for a set number of years. The bottom line is that one of the greatest risks retirees face today is not that of losing their money in risky investments, but that of outliving their money. Retirement income strategies must deal with this new reality.

Inflation

Inflation is another risk factor that retirees can't individually control. For previous generations of retirees, inflation was not much of an issue, because they generally lived for shorter amounts of time. With today's increased life expectancies, inflation is a real and serious threat to a successful retirement.

Inflation is the long-term tendency of money to lose purchasing power. It can have a particularly negative effect, because it chips away at retirement income by (1) increasing the future cost of goods and services, and (2) potentially eroding the value of dollars set aside to meet future costs. In 1970, for example, a gallon of milk cost $1.03. Today, the national average price for a gallon of milk is about $3.00,[2] and in 2030, a modest 3 percent inflation rate could send the price of milk to $5.58. As inflation increases the prices of everything from milk to new cars, it drives the buying power of a dollar down. If the rate of return on money invested between now and 2030 does not keep pace with inflation, the money used to pay for that $5.58 gallon of milk in the future will be worth much less than it is today. Therefore, not only will a gallon of milk cost more, but the money used to purchase it will also be worth less.

In order to clearly understand inflation, imagine an irrigation canal used to water a large farm. If, during a particular summer, the average temperature is five degrees warmer than past years, the farm may require more water. However, with higher temperatures, the water in the canal will evaporate more quickly. So not only does the farm require more water, but there is also less water to go around. Inflation works the same way.

The Consumer Price Index (CPI), created in 1967, is the tool that the government uses to monitor inflation. It does so by tracking the price of goods and services purchased by the average worker. According to the CPI, over the past forty-one years, the average annual inflation rate has been 4.55 percent, significantly higher in financial terms than the modest 3 percent used to illustrate the cost of milk in the above example (see fig. 1.2).

2. United States Department of Labor, Bureau of Labor Statistics, *CIP Detailed Report: Data for June 2009*, report prepared by Malik Crawford and Sanjeev Katz, June 2009.

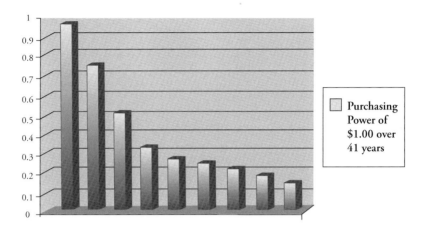

fig. 1.2
Source: Data from U.S. Bureau of Labor Statistics, *CPI-W, 1967-2008*

    To put inflation into perspective, $386,771 today has the same purchasing power as $60,000 did in 1967 (when the Consumer Price Index was created). The U.S. Department of Labor provides a handy CPI inflation calculator.[3]

    In the current environment of huge government budget deficits and spending, it is likely that inflation will continue to rise at least at the same pace as it has in recent history. In fact, many economic experts have predicted that inflation will likely soon exceed the comparatively low inflation rates of recent history. An additional inflation concern is health-care-related expenses. Retirees spend more on health care than does any other group, and inflation for health-care-related items is growing at double the national inflation rate.

    Given the one-two punch of longevity and inflation, it is imperative that retirees' savings include investments with the potential to beat inflation—especially considering the longer retirement many individuals face today.

---

3. The Consumer Price Index inflation calculator can be found at www.bls.gov/cpi.

Investment Risk

A significant number of retirees don't like managing their own investments, but with the decrease in traditional company-sponsored pension plans and the advent of the 401(k), everyone has become an investment manager, whether they like it or not.

The sad truth is that most people are not very good at it, either. A study done by Lipper and Dalbar compared the twenty-year average annual rate of return for stock mutual funds with the return realized by the average stock mutual fund investor. For the twenty years through 2008, the results were as follows (see fig. 1.3).

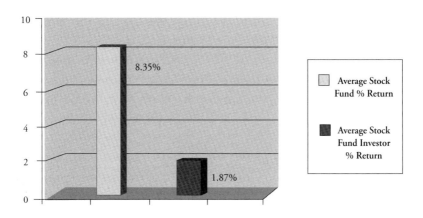

fig. 1.3

Although these two numbers bounced around a lot from year to year, the relationship between them remained constant. Over twenty years, the average stock fund investor managed to capture less than 25 percent of the return of the average stock fund. In essence, the average investor underperformed the average stock fund by 6 percent annually. Ouch! It is my belief that during this time period, the investors own behavior, which is most often based on irrational exuberance and equally irrational pessimism, ruled the day. It appears that the typical investor would follow the herd mentality, buying when stocks were high and selling in a panic when stocks were low. Seldom was he guided by a comprehensive investment plan, and little or no discipline was demonstrated. What is most concerning is that, for the most part, he failed at the easy part of investment management: the accumulation phase.

When people enter retirement, most of them also enter the distribution phase of investment management. In other words, they start withdrawing from investments. The distribution phase is much more difficult to manage than the accumulation phase, not only because it is crucial to know how to properly allocate and invest assets, but also because retirees need to know how to create a distribution plan that will provide a stream of income that will last until the end of their lives.

Complex investment choices as well as unprecedented market volatility has made it more difficult for the average investor to be successful in the distribution phase of investment management. Nothing short of a comprehensive income-distribution plan involving all sources of retirement income will assist you in providing the income needed to last for the rest of your life. The income distribution plan is the core of a financially sound retirement, but thus far, few retirees have adopted such a plan, and few financial professionals have had to create such a plan. It's something that will be unique to the baby boomer tsunami.[4]

---

4. Investing involves risk, including loss of principal. An investor's shares, when redeemed, may be worth less or more than the original investment price. An investor should carefully consider the investment objectives, risks, charges, and expenses of a mutual fund before investing. The fund prospectus contains this and other information about the fund. Contact your advisor or the fund company for a copy of the prospectus, which should be read carefully before investing.

CHAPTER 2

THE RETIREMENT
INCOME PLAN

D riving across the country without first looking at a map or a
GPS would be foolish. Likewise, you wouldn't think of going
on a vacation without booking hotels, purchasing airline tickets,
and studying a little about the destination. Why, then, would anyone attempt to navigate a possible thirty-year retirement without
a carefully thought-out retirement income plan? Thirty years is a
long time to live without a paycheck!

What Is a Retirement Income Plan?

A retirement income plan is a detailed blueprint that the retiree cre-
ates with a financial advisor. It helps you determine how to use your
assets to generate income that will last up to thirty years or more.
An optimally designed plan should produce an inflation-adjusted
income stream at the lowest possible risk and return the principal
to the retiree's spouse or children upon a retiree's death.

At Peterson Financial, we believe that every retiree and prere-
tiree (defined as those within five years of retirement) should have
a retirement income plan that realistically estimates expenses and

seeks to ensure that the retiree does not outlive his assets. There is a lot to consider as you transition from the accumulation of assets to the distribution of assets. Financially speaking, retirement is not a time to wing it; mistakes made early in retirement are unforgiving.

Some of the questions that need to be addressed in a retirement income plan are:

- Can I retire now, or should I wait?
- Will I be able to maintain my lifestyle?
- Will I be able to meet my inflation-adjusted expenses?
- From where will I receive income, and how much income will I be able to receive from all sources?
- When should my spouse and I apply for Social Security?
- How should my investments be allocated?
- How much income should I take from my investments? How much is too much?
- Will money be left over for my family upon my death?
- How do I pass excess money on at death in an efficient and tax-wise way?
- Which investment do I take income from now? Later?
- I still have a mortgage—is there a way to reduce or eliminate monthly payments?

Of course, no one can predict tomorrow, but a proper retirement income plan will better prepare the retiree to deal with future eventualities. A well-thought-out retirement income plan should seek to:

- Recognize and minimize the key retirement risks of longevity and inflation through proper investment management

- Identify expenses
- Identify and maximize all sources of income

Once you create and implement a plan, it's best to stick to it. If you don't follow it, you risk running out of money before running out of life.

Importance of Financial Discipline: Sheryl

Sheryl was a single schoolteacher, and through her hard work, she had accumulated a nice sum of money for retirement, which was invested in a well-diversified portfolio.

During the economic turmoil of 2008–2009, Sheryl spent a lot of time listening to "doom and gloom" talk shows and reading the all-too-abundant publications that pronounced the U.S. economy on the verge of a catastrophic collapse. She decided the only prudent thing to do was to liquidate her IRAs, pay off her home, and buy gold in preparation for Armageddon.

I explained to her the imprudence, both investment-wise and tax-wise, of her decision. The forces of financial misinformation, however, were too persuasive, and she followed through with her plan to liquidate. She determined that this was the right choice for her at the time. Six months later, during tax season, she called me and told me how foolish she had been for getting caught up in irrational fear at the time, especially now that she was trying to figure out how to pay a $60,000 tax bill incurred from the liquidation of her IRA.

What Is a Retirement Income Planner?

A retirement income planner is an investment advisor, specifically one who specializes in helping retirees manage and distribute their finances during retirement. Not all investment advisors are retirement income planners, but all retirement income planners are investment advisors. There is no governing body or professional designation for those who create these plans. In fact, anyone can call himself a retirement income planner. When planning your retirement, make sure the individual you hire to manage finances has indeed developed the skills necessary to create such a plan. From this point on, I will refer to those investment advisors who have developed income distribution competency as retirement income planners, in order to distinguish them from investment professionals who lack this expertise.

The Accumulator vs. the Distributor

Anyone who has ever been skiing will remember their first terrifying attempt at the sport. There are two different professionals at the ski resort to help the first-time skier: the lift operator and the ski instructor. The lift operator is responsible for running the lift machinery that gets an inexperienced skier to the top of the ski run, and for safely loading and unloading the skier onto and off of the lift. Few skiers get hurt while ascending the mountain on the lift; as long as they don't panic or lose patience and abandon the lift, they eventually make it to the top of the mountain.

Once the first-time skier arrives at the top of the run, the ski instructor takes over. The ski instructor's responsibilities include guiding the skier down the mountain, which is much more difficult than simply riding the lift up the mountain. You have to avoid the rocks, trees, and cliffs, and choose between steep, risky runs and easier, safer runs. The inexperienced skier is unfamiliar with the sometimes hazardous terrain, but the instructor knows the mountain and the risks, and can teach the new skier what needs to be done to arrive safely at the bottom of the ski run.

Think of the ski-lift operator as the person who helps accumulate funds for retiring, whether that person is a 401(k) consultant at work, an investment advisor, or even the retiree himself. As long as there are no major mistakes (like abandoning retirement funding altogether), the retiree will arrive at the retirement destination—though, obviously, some will be better prepared than others. The ski instructor, or the retirement income planner, must have more knowledge and expertise than the lift operator (the accumulator). Avoiding risky situations and guiding the retiree safely through retirement requires much more skill, discipline, and interaction with the retiree than does the accumulation of assets for retirement. Questions you'd never considered before will now become critical. How much income can be taken from investments? How should investments be allocated for income and inflation protection? Additionally, retirees will need to demonstrate patience and discipline to a degree they never exhibited during the accumulation stage of investment management. That is why a retirement income plan is so important.

Identifying Expenses

One of the hardest things about planning for retirement is determining how much income will be needed to last a lifetime. During my twenty-five years of retirement counseling, I've heard all sorts of generalized statements about what percentage of working wages will be necessary to maintain a financially viable retirement. I find most of these generalized assumptions or rules of thumb useless.

As discussed in chapter one, every individual is unique, and each has different financial needs and expectations regarding retirement. Simply put, I work with people who could retire wonderfully on $50,000 a year, while others could not retire on $50,000 a month. It all depends on the individual's chosen lifestyle and personal spending decisions.

Before you retire, it's important to estimate how much income you'll need. Keep in mind that expenses associated with working, such as professional clothing and transportation costs, will not be necessary for a retiree. Additionally, remember that there will be no more payroll deductions for 401(k) contributions, Medicare taxes, and FICA withholdings. On the other hand, it is likely that recreation costs will be higher for the young retiree, and that health care costs will be higher for the older retiree.

Estimating retirement expenses sounds easier than it really is. I've seen some people who can't realistically put together a true-to-life expense log until they've been retired for several months because they simply don't know how much money they will spend during retirement.[1] Expenses are only part of the equation, however, and once expenses are realistically identified, it is time to consider all current and future sources of income.

Identifying and Maximizing All Sources of Income

When you look at it from a financial perspective, retirement is really an income problem. Obviously, if income can stay ahead of expenses, all is well. If income can't stay ahead of expenses, you risk losing independence and dignity, and the dream of a carefree retirement turns into a nightmare. In my opinion, there are five major sources of retirement income:

1. Social Security
2. Company-sponsored pension plans
3. Employment during retirement
4. Reverse mortgages
5. Private investments

---

1. The intention of this book is not to spend a great deal of time on teaching the reader how to itemize expenses or create a budget. Free budgeting web sites are available online that do an excellent job of providing expense-tracking information and advice. Please see the list of additional resources at the end of the book for a list of recommended budgeting sites.

Once you identify these retirement income sources, the fun begins. The challenge is to figure out how to squeeze the most income from each of these sources during what could possibly be three decades.

The issues are very complex, and decisions in one category of retirement income will have an impact on other categories of income. For example, deciding to work past age sixty-two will have an impact on when you start Social Security. The decision of when and how to distribute a company-sponsored pension plan will affect which personal investments will need to be used for future income, as well as how and when they should be tapped. All retirement income decisions will have an impact on personal income tax rates.

The Dangers of Having No Plan: Larry

Larry was never a client of Peterson Financial, but he was referred to us after some mutual friends recognized that he needed some direction on his investments.

Larry, an engineer, was a very conservative investor during the 1990s. He didn't care about the big profits claimed by his colleagues in their 401(k)s; he was more comfortable keeping his money safe. Upon retirement, he happened to see one of his colleagues' 401(k) statements and figured out that he had made a huge mistake. His coworker, who had made the same salary as Larry and put into his 401(k) the same amount as Larry, had almost three times the money in his 401(k) because he aggressively invested in the booming stock market of the 1990s.

Understandably, Larry was sick. He was determined that from then on he was going to shift everything into stocks. At the time, Larry was sixty-four, and it was 1999. From 2000 to 2002, when the technology bubble burst, Larry lost over 50 percent of his already meager 401(k), at which time he shifted back into conservative investments, locking in his losses.

Larry had no plan, and, unfortunately, this is a common problem. Meeting with a financial advisor to discuss a plan and how to implement it would have saved Larry much stress and grief over his investments and perhaps helped Larry avoid the bad decisions that are now limiting his retirement income.

How Do I Put Together a Plan?

I don't expect that very many retirees could, should, or would even want to construct their own retirement income plan. There are always some people who will give it a valiant personal effort, though. These are the same people who would rather save twenty dollars making their own parachute than buy one from the factory. But my experience has been that most people recognize the need for professional financial advice when it comes to constructing a retirement income plan. It is virtually impossible for the average retiree to have the time and ability to fully understand the myriad questions he or she will face at retirement. You need a vast knowledge of tax laws, Social Security planning, investment allocation, pension plans, pension distribution rules, estate taxation rules, and investment distribution strategies, and you have to keep that knowledge up-to-date with the ever-changing investment, tax, and legal environments.

Searching for and finding a qualified retirement income planner requires careful effort, because they are hard to find. The truth is that there are very few financial professionals qualified or experienced enough to implement a retirement income plan. For example, investment professionals who have spent a lifetime helping people accumulate assets may not be knowledgeable enough to put together a viable income distribution plan, since their business was based on accumulation rather than distribution. Not to mention that they may have little or no knowledge of Social Security regulations, pension plans, IRS regulations regarding rollovers, required minimum distributions, or tax laws. The planning issues can be complex, and the decisions made at retirement are critically important. Today's financial decisions are unprecedented and unique to the baby boomer generation; there is simply no one-size-fits-all solution for today's retirees. The remainder of this book will review each source of income and give the reader some ideas and examples of how to manage and maximize the five sources of income: Social Security, company-sponsored pension plans, continued employment, reverse mortgages, and private investments.

CHAPTER 3

THE HISTORY AND FUTURE OF
SOCIAL SECURITY

The first source of income a retiree needs to know about is Social Security. It's an income source with a long history. Throughout time, different cultures have instituted varying forms of economic security for individuals. For the Greeks, it was olive oil, which was stockpiled for times of need, when people could sell it or consume it. Olive oil was a hot commodity in ancient Greece, transported in ships specially designed for the purpose. It was given in place of medals at Olympic games; indeed, individuals measured their wealth in oil, because it could always be traded for currency. In medieval Europe, the feudal system provided both military and economic security. Lords owned land and leased it to vassals, who in turn swore loyalty, pledged to protect and fight for their lord, and often paid taxes and offered a percentage of their crops to him. In this way, lords had both military security and economic security, and vassals had the security of land they could work and live off of.

No matter what shape economic security took, it was still of vital importance to the emotional and economical well-being of societies. As societies grew more complex, so did their governments and organizations. Among these organizations were those dedicated to preserving the economic security of their members. European guilds, the Freemasons, the Order of the Elks, and other fraternal societies regulated employment, provided financial assistance to members during hard times, and even implemented some of the first forms of life insurance.

Early American Methods of Financial Security

When the colonists arrived in America, they continued to follow the English poor law system: all relief for the less fortunate was a local responsibility, and any seen as "unworthy" were not granted financial support. As the colonies expanded and the government became more complex, it became obvious that the poor law system was no longer going to work. Instead of abolishing or reforming the system, however, colonists merely moved it to poorhouses and almshouses, where the poor were forced to live in order to receive aid. They hoped to make relief as unpleasant as possible, so as to discourage continued dependence upon the assistance of others. If you succumbed to poverty, your rights were stripped, your personal property was taken away, and you might be required to wear a *P* on your clothing to designate you as one of the poor.[1]

As the years passed, society at large realized that, for various reasons, including the civil rights abuses described above, the poorhouse system wasn't working either. They needed a new and better method for aiding those who had fallen upon hard times. Despite the apparent need for an organized system, it was not until the Great Depression that any lasting and aggressive action was taken to fix the problem.

---

1. William Trattner, *From Poor Law to Welfare State, 6th Edition: A History of Social Welfare in America*, 6th ed. (New York: The Free Press, 1999), 15-47.

The History of Social Security

Due to the lack of formal unemployment and poverty assistance, especially for the elderly, by the 1930s over half of all elderly Americans were living below the poverty level.[2] The country was in the throes of the Great Depression, and clearly, something needed to be done to assist all those who were unable to make ends meet or even to feed themselves.

According to the Social Security web site, there were four important changes to the fundamental demographics of America during this time which rendered previous forms of aid unworkable:

- The Industrial Revolution
- The urbanization of America
- The disappearance of the extended family
- A marked increase in life expectancy[3]

Fewer and fewer elderly Americans could count on their offspring for support; the Industrial Revolution had created an environment that allowed families to move away from each other, and they no longer depended upon each other for day-to-day assistance. By 1930, more people were living in cities than on farms.[4] They no longer grew their own food or lived in small, tight-knit communities. These changes meant that if a recession, a layoff, or a business failure hit unexpectedly, individuals would not have their land or their farming to provide them with at least the bare minimum of sustenance.[5]

---

2. Social Security Administration, *Historical Background and Development of Social Security*, http://www.ssa.gov/history/briefhistory3.html.

3. Ibid.

4. Ibid.

5. Daniel Beland, *Social Security: History and Politics from the New Deal to the Privatization Debate* (Kansas: University Press of Kansas, 2007), 49-51.

When the stock market crash of 1929 occurred, America was at its most fragile, since the traditional forms of economic security, land and family, were no longer in place. Previously, if one family member fell on hard times, the extended family would help out until the issue was resolved and the family member was returned to solvency. Now, however, the families were not together and could not pitch in to help each other over great distances.

Numerous ideas for solving the problem of poverty, some more radical than others, were discussed throughout the 1930s. The three top contenders were to rely on volunteerism, to expand welfare, and to ignore the problem because it was likely just a short economic dip. Each of these solutions presented problems of its own. Ignoring the problem only made it worse, as it became more apparent that the Depression would last longer than a year or two. Volunteerism had been successful in the past, but that had been at a time when America as a nation was economically strong. Now the entire nation had lost roughly one-third of its wealth, and there was neither money nor food for others to provide on a volunteer basis.[6] As for expanding welfare, the current plans were woefully inadequate, and to expand them to levels that would provide tangible relief would require much more money and effort than was possible for the United States at that time.

It was then that President Franklin D. Roosevelt was elected to office and presented the idea of a "social insurance," program, much like the social insurance programs that had been operating in several European countries for quite some time. This idea caught on quickly and banished all of the radical "share the wealth" ideas, as well as the idea of expanding welfare. Only now that confidence in the majority of American institutions was shaken—and, in some cases, shattered—could the nation accept and implement social insurance. The program that was created would become known as Social Security.[7]

---

6. Ibid, 53-55.
7. Social Security Administration, *Historical Background and Development of*

What Is Social Security?

Social Security was created in 1937 to act as social insurance for the elderly, specifically the elderly poor. There are several parts to the system, but the most significant one is Old-Age, Survivors, and Disability Insurance (OASDI). OASDI benefits are funded through payroll taxes on both employees and employers.

Implementing the new Social Security system was a daunting task. First of all, there were committees to be formed to oversee the Social Security system and its trust fund. Second, Social Security numbers needed to be given to all employers and workers so their earnings and credits could be tracked to determine the monthly benefits they'd receive once they retired. Those who had not worked long enough to benefit from the system when it was implemented (i.e., those who were already near retirement) received a lump-sum payment when they retired, based on how much they had put into the system. The average lump-sum payment at this time was around $58. Ernest Ackerman, who retired the day after Social Security was implemented, paid $0.05 into the system and received $0.17 for his lump sum.[8]

Monthly benefits began in January 1940. The first check, for $22.54, went to Ida May Fuller. Ida Fuller received this same amount each month until Cost of Living Adjustments (COLAs) were enacted in 1950, at which point her checks included a yearly increase. Ida Fuller lived to be one hundred, well beyond the life expectancy for her generation; she definitely profited from the Social Security system over her lifetime. From January 1940 until today, workers who are eligible for Social Security, their spouses, and qualifying ex-spouses, have received checks to supplement their retirement incomes.[9]

Social Security, under "The Social Insurance Movement," http://www.ssa.gov /history/briefhistory3.html; Daniel Beland, *Social Security,* 81, 87.

8. Social Security Administration, *Historical Background,* under "First Payments," http://www.ssa.gov/history/briefhistory3.html.

9. Elaine Floyd, CFP, *The Financial Advisor's Guide to Savvy Social Security Planning for Boomers* (New York: Horsesmouth, 2009), 150.

How Important Is Social Security to Retirees Today?

Social Security was never meant to be the sole source of income for retirees, and, on average, it provides only around 40 percent of retirement income today. The other 60 percent must come from personal savings, IRAs, corporate pensions, and employment. In fact, the higher the wages you earn during your working years, the more income you will need to replace from sources other than Social Security. The system was purposely designed to provide more assistance to lower-income workers, who didn't have as much opportunity to create large nest eggs for retirement, in order to lessen widespread poverty during retirement.

However, because Social Security does provide up to 40 percent of income during retirement, it can be a very important part of the retirement planning process. A person's total Social Security income throughout retirement is probably far greater than most people realize. For example, if a person earned the maximum yearly earnings for Social Security throughout life, and waited until full retirement age (FRA) to apply for benefits, they'd receive $378,786 over the first ten years of retirement. If that person lived thirty years into retirement, they'd receive $1,444,796. These numbers are adjusted to include the annual COLAs (Cost-of-living adjustments) at an assumed rate of 2.8 percent. COLAs are added each year to help retirees keep up with inflation, and have averaged around 3 percent. While 3 percent seems relatively small, over the long term COLAs can increase Social Security benefits substantially, especially if the recipient chooses to delay benefits.

Social Security provides a firm foundation on which to create a retirement income plan. It is guaranteed income–like paychecks from a regular job, it can be depended upon for a lifetime, and you know what amount you'll receive before you receive it, which makes the planning process easier. Furthermore, benefits are infla-tion-adjusted on a yearly basis, which usually provides yearly pay increases.[10] Survivors and dependents can also count on continued payments in the form of survivor benefits after the primary worker dies. For these reasons, Social Security planning and maximization are key components of any sound retirement income plan.

Will Social Security Be There for Me?

One of the big questions revolving around Social Security today is whether or not it will be there for people retiring in the near future. As baby boomers enter retirement, the ratio of workers to retirees will sharply decline and continue to decline through 2050, which has led many to fear that there will not be enough money entering the system to offset the money leaving the system.

From the beginning, Social Security was designed as a pay-as-you-go system; money was paid into a trust fund, and immediately paid out to current retirees. The trust fund was never expected to accumulate large reserves; it was designed to provide just enough excess to cover payments. Roosevelt planned Social Security to be self-financing—in fact, it is against the law for Social Security to borrow money from the government in order to cover its bills.[11]

According to the 2010 Congressional Budget Office report,[12] Social Security's revenues are currently greater than its payments due to the large number of baby boomers in the work force, many of whom have high-paying jobs and therefore contribute large sums to the system each year. But as the baby boomer generation begins to retire at a rate of nearly 365 per hour, payments will begin to exceed revenues starting in 2016. This does not mean, however, that payments will be impossible to meet. In 2016, Social Security will have its trust fund and securities to fall back on. But these will

---

10. For 2010, there will be a zero percent COLA because inflation did not rise in 2009. Social Security benefits increased by a 5.8 percent COLA in 2009.

11. Ibid, 149.

12. Congressional Budget Office, The Long-Term Budget Outlook, "The Long Term Outlook for Social Security, August 2010; 47-52.

be exhausted in 2039, at which time Social Security will only have the funds and the legal authority to pay 76 percent of the projected benefits. It therefore appears that in the immediate future Social Security is secure, but adjustments will have to be made to ensure Social Security benefits for future generations.[13]

The Congressional Budget Office releases an annual report describing the financial health of Social Security, and the numbers in the report fluctuate from year to year. They issue these reports so that Congress will have enough warning to gradually implement changes and restore balance in the system. It is likely that by the time the trust fund and securities are exhausted in 2037, a solution will have been implemented. Some of the possible solutions include increasing the Social Security tax by 1.7 percent, reducing the annual COLAs, increasing the limit on taxable yearly earnings, or raising the retirement age (as has been done in the past). Using one of these possible modifications would return the Social Security system to actuarial balance.

The media has created something of a panic, stating that Social Security is going bankrupt and will not be able to meet obligations in the coming years. Furthermore, Social Security becomes a hot topic during election years because many politicians know their stance can be a deciding factor for many voters. Because of this, Social Security has been front and center in media and politics over the last decade. Despite all the noise, however, you can rely on Social Security to provide a solid foundation for your retirement.

13. Social Security Board of Trustees, *The 2009 Annual Report of the Board of Trustees of the Federal Old-Age and Survivors Insurance and Federal Disability Insurance Trust Funds.* 11 ong., 1ˢᵗ sess., 2009. H. Doc. 111-41, 8–20.

CHAPTER 4

THE INS AND OUTS OF
SOCIAL SECURITY

P eople miss out on millions of dollars in benefits each year because they don't understand Social Security. In particular, many people are unaware of their eligibility for spousal benefits, divorced spouse benefits, and survivor benefits, which can substantially increase Social Security benefits over a lifetime.

For this reason, a retirement income plan that includes maximizing Social Security benefits can be a lifesaver. The question is, who is going to help you develop a maximization plan when it is often difficult to find a CPA, attorney, or even a financial planner with adequate knowledge of Social Security? Social Security workers are more than willing to help, but anyone who has been to a local Social Security office has seen the burden that they are under. Because of their workload, not a lot of customized Social Security planning happens there. They can provide you with the basic numbers—your benefit amount at sixty-two, at full retirement age, and at seventy—but they can't devote much time or consideration to explaining break-even points or potential gains and losses based upon age at application. Imagine how much worse that situation will be once the majority of the eighty million baby boomers retire.

Although Social Security workers want recipients to receive as much money as possible, they can't know everyone's personal financial situation, and they don't have the time to create a Social Security maximization plan. This is where a Social-Security-savvy advisor comes in handy. In fact, let me emphasize that maximizing Social Security only happens with a qualified retirement income planner who understands how Social Security works.

This chapter will go over some of the major provisions of Social Security, which are complicated in and of themselves, but which will hopefully provide the reader with a basic understanding of which questions to ask when meeting with a retirement income planner. **The maximization and distribution scenarios in this chapter have not taken individual cash flow or health concerns into consideration, but these would need to be addressed prior to creating a Social Security distribution plan.** I therefore suggest that the reader ask a retirement income planner to create a customized Social Security maximization report. I've done my very best to simplify the information within this chapter, but there's a limited amount of simplification that can be done. After all, how simple can a program that was created and administered by politicians for the last eighty years be?

When Should I File?

The big question when it comes to Social Security planning is when retirees should apply. Most are told (and most believe) that they should apply as early as possible, at age sixty-two, in order to get the most out of the system. However, this is usually not the best idea when trying to maximize lifetime benefits. A general rule is that the longer benefits are put off, the larger the monthly check will be—and with a larger check, you'll eventually receive more benefits than you would have if you'd taken your benefits early.

Though there is no one-size-fits-all answer to this question, there are general guidelines that almost any healthy retiree can follow. With the help of an advisor, you can develop a plan suited to individual needs. Some retirees should absolutely wait until age seventy to apply for benefits, because they're still working or simply don't need the money yet. Others who need the money now or who are in poor health could gain more from taking benefits early, despite the common drawbacks. No matter what category you fall into, don't blindly follow the 72 percent of Americans who file at age sixty-two just because it's the youngest filing age. The decision of when to file for Social Security benefits is irreversible, and it can make a difference of many thousands of dollars in benefits paid during a lifetime. This is not a decision to take lightly!

How Benefits Are Calculated

Anyone who has worked in a Social-Security-covered job for at least ten years is eligible for Social Security, but benefits are based upon the highest thirty-five years of earnings and the age at which benefits are first received. So, if you took a couple of years off, it is a good idea to work until you have at least thirty-five years to draw from. Also, if a current job pays well, working a couple years longer rather than retiring right away can greatly increase your future benefits by replacing low-earning years.

Deciding when to apply for benefits can be tricky, but a general rule of thumb is to wait until at least full retirement age (see fig. 4.1), or until age seventy. Applying at an earlier age results in a lower monthly benefit, while applying at a later age (after full retirement age through age seventy) results in a higher monthly benefit. Postponing benefits after age seventy is useless, because benefits do not accrue delayed credits after that time.

AGE WHEN YOU ARE ELIGIBLE TO RECEIVE FULL SOCIAL SECURITY BENEFITS	
YEAR OF BIRTH	**FULL RETIREMENT AGE (FRA)**
1937 OR EARLIER	65
1938	65 and 2 months
1939	65 and 4 months
1940	65 and 6 months
1941	65 and 8 months
1942	65 and 10 months
1943 - 1954	66
1955	66 and 2 months
1956	66 and 4 months
1957	66 and 6 months
1958	66 and 8 months
1959	66 and 10 months
1960 OR LATER	67

fig. 4.1
Source: courtesy of Social Security Administration, *Full Retirement Age*

Those who take Social Security at age sixty-two, the earliest age eligible for Social Security, will only receive 75 percent of their benefits to compensate for the fact that they will receive more checks if they live until the average life expectancy. Those who collect at their full retirement age will receive 100 percent of benefits, while those who delay benefits until age seventy will receive 132 percent of their benefits each month (see fig. 4.2).

AMOUNT OF BENEFIT AT DIFFERENT AGES		
AGE BENEFITS ARE CLAIMED	% OF BENEFIT	BENEFIT IN TODAY'S DOLLARS IF BENEFIT AT FULL RETIREMENT AGE IS $ 2200
62 (earliest)	75.00%	$ 1,650
63	80.00	$ 1,760
64	86.67	$ 1,907
65	93.33	$ 2,053
66 (FRA)	100.00	$ 2,200
67	108.00	$ 2,376
68	116.00	$ 2,552
69	124.00	$ 2,728
70 (maximum)	132.00	$ 2,904

fig. 4.2

Over time, the extra 32 percent will compound with annual COLAs and provide you with more income than you would have received had you applied for benefits at an earlier age. The point at which this happens is called the *break-even age*, and the best way to decide when to start receiving Social Security benefits is to perform a *break-even analysis*. The basic goal of this analysis is to figure out how long it would take to catch up if you collected benefits later rather than earlier. The break-even age is often in your mid to late seventies. If the projected life expectancy of the husband or the wife exceeds the break-even age, it is best to put off applying for benefits for as long as possible, up to age seventy.

For example, say Larry and Glen are both entitled to $1,900 a month at their full retirement age, but Larry decides to apply for his benefit at age sixty-two, receiving $1,425 a month, or 75 percent of his full benefit. Glen decides to wait until his full retirement age, sixty-six. From age sixty-two to age sixty-six, Larry will receive $68,400 before Glen even starts receiving benefits. But because Glen will be receiving a larger monthly check, he will eventually catch up to Larry and receive more in the long run. According to a breakeven analysis, at age seventy-eight Glen will begin receiving more money from the system than Larry. As discussed in chapter 1, today's retirees have a very good chance of living into their nineties. Therefore, under normal circumstances, people who can wait to apply for benefits should do so.

Spousal Planning

Social Security planning can become complicated when spouses are factored in. The goal is to maximize the benefits that a couple will receive for as long as at least one of them is living. Many don't realize that either spouse can collect a spousal benefit; spousal benefits are not restricted to the lower-earning spouse. While keeping in mind that spousal benefits are gender neutral, for ease of explanation, I'll refer to the higher earner as the husband and the lower earner as the wife. I realize this stereotype is no longer accurate in many cases, but it will make my explanations more concise.

A spousal benefit is equal to half of the other spouse's full benefit. For example, a wife who never worked outside the home could collect half of her husband's benefit. If Brent were eligible for $1,890 each month, his wife Mary could collect an additional $945. If Mary had worked enough to be eligible for benefits, she would receive whichever was greater: her own benefit, or her spousal benefit. So if Mary's own benefit was, say, $675, she would still receive the spousal benefit, because it is greater than her own benefit. However, if her own benefit were, for example, $1,100, she would receive her own benefit rather than her spousal benefit.

Spousal benefits are subject to reduced monthly benefits if you apply for them early, so waiting until full retirement age to apply for spousal benefits is generally the best option. Waiting beyond this age doesn't make sense, however, because maximum spousal benefits are based on the worker's benefit amount at full retirement age, *not* on the benefit received if the spouse waits until the age of seventy. While Brent could receive a greater benefit by waiting until age seventy to apply for Social Security, Mary's spousal benefit would not increase if she waited until age seventy to collect it; spousal benefits do not accrue delayed credits. Therefore, Mary should wait to collect her spousal benefit until full retirement age (sixty-six) if possible, but waiting past age sixty-six would be pointless.

The potential penalties of applying early for a spousal benefit are two-fold. First, if Mary applied for her spousal benefit prior to full retirement age, she would receive a permanent reduced benefit. Second, this reduced benefit would apply not only to her spousal benefit, but also to her own benefit if she decided to switch to that later. For this reason, it is generally best not to apply for any spousal benefits before full retirement age. To maximize family income and ensure a larger survivor benefit, the higher-earning spouse should delay benefits until age seventy, regardless of health status. This is because the higher of the two spouses' benefits will be awarded to the survivor, regardless of which spouse passes away first.

The rules for spousal benefits are diverse and complicated. I have tried to simplify them to give the reader a general idea of what spousal benefits are and how they can be collected in order to maximize benefits. An appointment with a retirement income planner to run various Social Security distribution scenarios is highly recommended. There are different strategies for creating a maximization plan to provide the couple with the most money by taking spousal benefits and their own benefits at different times. Customized analyses are needed for each situation in order to determine the best path for each couple.

Spousal Planning: Brian and Katie

Katie is an administrator at a hospital, while Brian, her husband, owns a construction company. Both have reached their full retirement age of sixty-six.

Brian has always made more money than Katie and has a longer work history, so he qualified for the greater Social Security benefit. If both took their benefits at age sixty-six, Brian would receive $2,125, and Katie would receive $1,260. However, this would not maximize the amount they could receive together.

I suggested a better strategy would be for Brian to "file and suspend" his benefit so that Katie can apply for her spousal benefit based upon Brian's earnings. Katie would need to limit the scope of her application to Brian's spousal benefit so her own earnings record would not be taken into account, and by doing so Katie would receive $1,063 starting at age sixty-six. This allows both of them to delay taking their own benefits until age seventy, at which time Brian's benefit would be $3,133 and Katie's would be $1,857, assuming an annual COLA of 2.8%.

By doing so, they'd start receiving more cumulative benefits at age seventy-seven. If both lived to age eighty-five, they'd receive an extra $171,070 in Social Security benefits than they would have if they had both filed at age 66. In addition, if Brian predeceases Katie, she would receive a much larger survivor benefit.

It is important to note that in order for a wife to collect spousal benefits, the husband has to have filed with Social Security. If the husband has not reached age seventy and would like to wait to receive his maximum benefits, he can *file and suspend* as long as he is at least of full retirement age; before that, he is ineligible for this option. Many Social Security workers are not aware of this possibility, though it was included in the Senior Citizens' Freedom to Work Act of 2000. Filing and suspending (filing in the month a retiree reaches FRA and suspending benefits) puts the husband on the Social Security rolls so his wife can claim spousal benefits, but also allows the accumulation of delayed credits on his record until he turns seventy. Again, this rule is gender neutral; a wife can also file and suspend so her husband can collect a spousal benefit while she holds off on receiving benefits.

Survivorship Planning

When people are deciding when to apply for Social Security, they often overlook the idea of survivor benefits. Many don't realize that survivor benefits are built into the Social Security system, and those benefits are becoming increasingly important as medical advances increase life expectancies. Usually, husbands die first due to gender discrepancies in life expectancies; women tend to live five to six years longer than men. Because of this, it is important for the higher-earning spouse to delay applying for benefits for as long as possible to ensure a higher survivor benefit.

Survivor benefits, unlike spousal benefits, provide the full amount of the higher-earning spouse's benefit. If Jerry receives $2,100 each month, and his wife, Margaret, receives $1,250 each month, when Jerry dies, Margaret will start receiving Jerry's $2,100 in place of her $1,250. She will continue to receive this higher amount, including any annual COLAs, until she dies. It is important to note that you cannot collect a survivor benefit and your own benefit at the same time—the higher one will prevail unless you request to continue receiving the smaller benefit to allow the other to accrue delayed credits, a strategy that will be discussed shortly.

One of the main reasons why the higher-earning spouse should delay receiving Social Security until age seventy is that the survivor benefit is equal to the actual benefit paid out, not to the benefit that would be received at full retirement age. This means that if Jerry receives $2,100 at full retirement age, he would receive $2,772 at age seventy. As long as he waits to apply until age seventy, Margaret will be left with that $2,772 survivor benefit.

Survivor benefits are also subject to the reduced monthly benefit rule if collected before full retirement age, but, unlike spousal benefits, that reduction *does not impose itself upon the survivor's own benefit*. This means that Margaret could collect her survivor benefit early if she needed it, and then switch to her own benefit at age seventy after it has grown. The reverse is also true. Margaret could take her own benefit early and switch to her survivor benefit at sixty-six. Like spousal benefits, survivor benefits do not grow beyond age sixty-six, so there is no point in delaying them.

Opportunity Lost: Gary and Elizabeth

Gary worked in the manufacturing industry, and before Elizabeth died, she worked as a nurse administrator at a local hospital.

Gary didn't understand that he could receive survivor Social Security benefits as the spouse of a deceased person who had paid into the Social Security system. Therefore, instead of applying for a survivor benefit based on Elizabeth's earnings, Gary applied for his own reduced benefit at age sixty-two. A Social Security recipient cannot collect both a survivor benefit and his own benefit—only the greater of the two.

I brought this mistake to his attention and showed him that he could have let his benefit grow to age seventy while at the same time receiving a survivor benefit on Elizabeth's record, which would have increased his monthly Social Security income from $1,300 to $2,145 at age seventy.

We contacted the Social Security office and were told that Gary would have to refund all the Social Security payments he had ever received in order to recalculate his payment using Elizabeth's survivor benefit. Unfortunately, Gary did not have access to sufficient cash to refund the Social Security Administration; therefore he is stuck with the current reduced payment for the rest of his life and will never benefit from Elizabeth's thirty years of contributions to Social Security.

Maximizing a Future Survivor Benefit: Mark and Judy

Mark and Judy were a wealthy couple who earned their wealth by turning orchards into subdivisions. Despite their wealth, Mark started taking his Social Security at age sixty-two. He wanted to "get as much back from the system as possible," and besides, his health was declining. The monthly Social Security income of $1,828 was not necessary for Mark and Judy at the time, but it would become necessary when Mark died. Judy was only fifty-six and in good health, while Mark was six years older and in poor health.

At the time, Judy's survivor benefit was the monthly $1,828 that Mark received. If Mark had waited to take his Social Security until age seventy, his monthly benefit and Judy's survivor benefit would have been $4,012, assuming an annual 2.8% COLA. While Mark did not have a long life expectancy, Judy did. If he were to die at seventy-one and she were to live to age ninety, his delay in taking his benefit until age seventy would result in $628,044 extra in benefits over Judy's lifetime.

We discovered this difference in benefits soon after Mark began taking Social Security benefits, so we were able to contact Social Security and stop the benefit—deferring it until he reaches the age of seventy.

While we advocate that the higher-earning spouse wait until age seventy to apply for benefits, we realize this is not feasible for everyone. This is why Social Security planning is such a vital part of a retirement income plan. If Social Security benefits are needed early and cannot be maximized for survivors, another source of retirement income can take over that role. However, it is my job to point out how best to maximize Social Security, and having the higher-earning spouse wait until age seventy to apply is the best scenario for both the husband and the wife, regardless of who dies first.

It is important to note that survivor benefits can also be claimed on a deceased ex-spouse's earnings record. The rules of ex-spouse survivor benefits are the same as the rules for widows and widowers.

Divorced Spouse Benefits

As with spousal benefits for married couples, you can claim a spousal benefit on an ex-spouse's earning record if the benefit would be higher than your own benefit. For continued ease of explanation, we are going to assume that the wife is claiming benefits on an ex-husband's record, but remember that divorced spouse benefits are available to both sexes. In order to qualify, a woman claiming the benefit must meet general eligibility requirements and must have been married to her ex-husband for at least ten years. If she has multiple ex-husbands, she will receive the highest benefit from among those marriages. (In the opposite scenario, a man with multiple ex-wives may end up with multiple benefit claims on his record.)

The ex-husband is not notified if a former spouse requests a benefit based on his earnings record, nor does it affect his own benefit. Unlike spousal benefits, the divorced husband does not need to have applied for his own benefit before an ex-wife can claim a divorced spouse benefit, but he does need to meet general eligibility requirements for Social Security (i.e., age sixty-two or older, with an earnings record from which FICA taxes were withheld.)

To qualify to receive a divorced spouse benefit, the ex-wife must either (1) be currently unmarried, or (2) have waited until *after age sixty* to re-marry. If she remarries prior to age sixty, divorced spouse benefits are not an option; only a spousal benefit on the current husband's record is available to her. If she remarries after age sixty and is already receiving divorced spouse benefits, that benefit will not be affected. She can switch to a spousal benefit on her current husband's record if it is higher, or she can continue receiving her divorced spouse benefit.

Divorced Spouse Benefit: Amy

Amy was a single retiree who had been married to her ex-husband for over twenty years before they divorced. She had not spent a full thirty-five years in the workforce and didn't have a full earnings record on which to base Social Security payments, so her Social Security payments were understandably small.

When she reached age sixty-six, she filed for her Social Security benefits, receiving $955 per month. I suggested to her that we should take a trip to the Social Security office and see whether her divorced spouse benefit would be higher than her current full benefit.

Her husband had been a general practitioner and had a very respectable earnings history, earning nearly the maximum Social Security earnings each year. It turned out that her divorced spouse benefit, 50 percent of his benefit, would amount to $1,345. Amy is now receiving this higher benefit and her retirement is more comfortable.

Working While Receiving Benefits

For the majority of baby boomers, full retirement age will be sixty-six or sixty-seven. Baby boomers who plan to continue working until at least this age should not apply for early benefits. This is because if Social Security is collected from ages sixty-two through full retirement age, all earnings are subject to an *earnings test*: for every two dollars earned over a certain amount ($14,160 in 2011), one dollar is withheld in benefits. This helps make up for the fact that benefits are being taken when (1) they aren't necessarily needed, and (2) credits for future Social Security payments are still being accrued through work. If you make enough money (and the threshold will change from year to year, so it's best to visit your retirement income planner or the Social Security office or website to determine the earnings test amount for the current year), all benefits will be withheld. If all your benefits are being withheld anyway, there's no point in applying for them and subjecting yourself to a permanently reduced benefit for life.

The year that you reach full retirement age, you can earn more income ($37,680 in 2011) before withholdings begin (at the rate of one dollar withheld for every three dollars earned) until the month that you reach full retirement age. Once you reach full retirement age, no more Social Security will be withheld, regardless of your earnings. For example, if you were turning sixty-six on May 6, you could earn up to $37,680 between January and May 6 without having Social Security withheld. On May 6, that limit will be removed and you can earn as much as you want from that point forward.

Because of these earning maximums, anyone who plans to continue working in a high-paying position should delay collecting benefits until at least sixty-six to avoid having benefits withheld. Although withheld benefits will eventually be paid back when you reach full retirement age, you can never recover the reduction in benefits from applying for benefits early. So, it's best to wait to apply for Social Security until after your working years are over.

Social Security Taxation

If you choose to work and collect Social Security benefits at the same time, be aware that those benefits are not only subject to the reduction described above, but also to taxation. According to law, if a person's total income plus half of his benefits is more than the base amount decided by Congress in 1983 and 1993, a certain amount of Social Security benefits will be taxable. However, these thresholds were never indexed for inflation, so today even moderate-income households are subject to this taxation.

The laws and formulas for taxation of Social Security benefits are complicated and take many different situations into consideration. For this reason, if you continue to work, it's advisable not to apply for benefits until you're finished working. Otherwise, talking to a tax professional and a financial planner to discuss the specifics of Social Security taxation is recommended.

A Note About Medicare

Regardless of when you first collect Social Security benefits, you need to apply for Medicare at age sixty-five. If you don't apply for it in a timely manner (I recommended starting the application process three months before turning sixty-five), a 10 percent penalty will be added to the Part B premium for each twelve-month period that you wait. For example, if you apply at age sixty-seven, a 20 percent penalty is added to the Part B premium for the rest of your life. If you don't apply for Medicare within the appropriate time frame, you'll have to wait for the open enrollment period the following year, which happens from January 1 through March 31.

There are always exceptions to the rule, though, and the big exception in this case is that if a sixty-five-year-old is still working, he can wait to apply until after retiring with no penalty. When he does retire, he will have eight months to complete the application for Medicare before the 10 percent penalty will be added. If you apply for Social Security benefits before age sixty-five, Medicare will automatically start. Otherwise, you have to apply separately within the time frame discussed above.

The five most important things to remember about Medicare are:

1. **Medicare is not automatic.** Everyone has to sign up within a specific period of time (unless you're receiving Social Security benefits early, in which case Medicare will automatically kick in at age sixty-five).

2. **Medicare will not start until age sixty-five.** Regardless of whether you collect Social Security benefits before age sixty-five, Medicare will not start until then. If you don't have employer coverage, you'll need private health insurance to cover the gap.

3. **Medicare is not free.** Its cost is deducted monthly from your Social Security payments, and it doesn't cover everything. It's a good idea to have supplemental insurance to cover costs that Medicare doesn't.

4. **Medicare supplemental insurance (Medigap) is available.** However, it also costs money, and you have to apply for it within a specific time period. Medigap is sold by private insurance companies. Medicare.gov has a list of the policies available, including their prices and features. You can shop for Medigap plans according to the medications you are taking.

5. **Medicare does not cover long-term care.** Long-term care insurance must be purchased separately from a private insurance company.

Summary

Social Security is a valuable retirement income asset. You should manage it carefully, as you would any other asset, in order to maximize its benefits. A little time and effort can pay significant dividends when you're deciding when and how to receive your benefits. The rules and regulations can be daunting, but with proper planning Social Security can provide years of guaranteed income and can be the foundation of a retirement income plan.

The rumors that the Social Security system is going broke have helped motivate baby boomers to save for their retirement. This is a good thing; many baby boomers will have a more comfortable retirement, plus money to hedge against any unforeseen emergencies. But baby boomers do stand to receive a substantial amount of their retirement income from Social Security, especially if they have had a solid earnings history. While you can't fund your retirement with Social Security alone, it's definitely enough to help provide a stable income during retirement, if you plan it properly and carefully.

CHAPTER 5

THE VANISHING PENSION

There was a time when retirement planning was little more than a hearty handshake and a predictable pension check from your employer. Though that pension income wasn't adjusted for inflation, it provided a guaranteed income. Retirement income was made up of a three-legged stool: corporate pensions, Social Security, and personal savings. You could count on two-thirds of your retirement income from Social Security and pensions ("mailbox money," as I liked to refer to it, because it predictably arrived in the mail every month).

Baby boomers don't have that luxury; corporate pensions, sometimes called *defined benefit plans*, are an endangered species. Today, less than one-third of retirement income is generated by these pension plans. Instead, many retirees are balancing their retirement on an uneven, two-legged stool: Social Security and personal investments. Pensions are being replaced by defined contribution plans, usually in the form of 401(k)s. If you're one of the few people lucky enough to have a pension, continue reading to see how pension planning can aid in a successful retirement income plan. If this won't be one of your sources of income, feel free to skip ahead to the next chapter.

> **Defined Benefit Plan:** Better known as a pension; a company retirement plan in which a retired employee receives a specific amount each month based on salary history and years of service, and in which the employer bears the investment risk and the employee pays nothing into the pension.
>
> **Defined Contribution Plan:** Better known as a 401(k); a company retirement plan, such as a 401(k) plan or 403(b) plan, in which the employee elects to defer some amount of his/her salary into the plan and bears the investment risk.

The Defined Benefit Pension Plan

Previously, the majority of workers built their lives and careers around a single company, and were rewarded for their lifetime loyalty with a pension plan at retirement. Some pensions could be taken as a lump sum, others as a monthly benefit that was expected to last until the death of the retiree. The decline of the defined benefit retirement plan, or pension, began in the 1970s, when the government tried to rectify certain abuses by passing the Employee Retirement Income Security Act (ERISA).

While ERISA has deflected the majority of corporate abuses over the years (namely the dismissal of employees a couple of months short of their pension eligibility date), it also introduced many complicated laws that are hard to comply with. To avoid dealing with the politics and complexities of ERISA, many companies decided to do away with pension plans. They were never a mandatory offering for companies anyway, and it was easier to drop them than to conform to the new regulations. In 1985, there were 114,000 defined benefit retirement plans in the United States; today there are only 38,000.

For employers, these plans are an expensive undertaking. Companies that offer pension plans must, by law, provide current retirees with their predetermined retirement benefit every month, even if the investment fund that the pensions are paid from has done poorly. This is another one of the main reasons why corporate America has done away with the traditional pension in recent years—pension payments, especially during turbulent economic times, have the potential to put a company out of business. Simply stated, most companies view the risk and difficulty of maintaining a defined benefit pension plan as not worth the effort. Again, if you have a defined benefit pension plan, consider yourself fortunate.

The New Pension

While the traditional pension plan has dwindled, a new employer-sponsored retirement plan has been on the rise: the 401(k). These plans are cheaper to fund for employers and cheaper to administer. Employees seem to be benefiting from the 401(k) as well, especially considering the mobility of contemporary American society. Now that employees change jobs on a more frequent basis, the 401(k) allows them to take their money with them from job to job and continue contributing to it. With a traditional defined benefit pension, this would be impossible. In the past, workers saw the rewards of their loyalty to a company; today, workers rarely devote a lifetime to one company, because frankly, there are no rewards for their devotion. According to a survey by the Employee Benefits Research Institute (EBRI), workers in 2002 stayed with companies for an average of 4.7 years, much lower than the averages for previous generations[1].

So as traditional pensions become harder to fund and harder to find, 401(k)s are taking their place. While a defined benefit pension

---

1. Employee Benefit Research Institute, *EBRI General Benefits Research: Findings 2003*, under "Employee Tenure," http://www.ebri.org/media/findings/.

plan promises a specific monthly sum after retirement, a defined contribution plan (401(k)), does not. In these plans, an employee adds money to the account, and the employer has the option to "match" the contribution usually at a predetermined rate (e.g., up to 3 to 5 percent of the employee's salary). While 401(k) plans offer flexibility for today's mobile society, they do shift the majority of the retirement burden to the employee rather than the employer, making financial discipline even more important.

Unlike pension plans, 401(k)s fluctuate in value based on market conditions, making it impossible to determine how much income per month these plans will generate for retirement. Once you retire, you can roll the 401(k) into an IRA and incorporate the IRA into a comprehensive retirement income plan.

The Pension Distribution Plan

Those who do have a defined benefit plan will have an added dimension to their retirement planning. They face several irrevocable decisions upon retirement. These decisions must be navigated carefully to maximize the pension distribution.

1. Should I roll my pension into an IRA and manage the money myself, or should I leave the money in the company pension plan in order to guarantee a monthly income?

2. How do I maximize my monthly income for both myself and my spouse?

The Pension Rollover

About half of all pension plans allow only a monthly income payment. But if the retiree does have the option of rolling a lump-sum pension into an IRA, he or she should strongly consider it. While monthly payments guarantee income and reduce exposure to market risk, they prevent your money from growing in a retirement account. In contrast, an IRA puts you in charge of your own money and financial destiny. You, not the pension plan, decide how your money is invested and distributed.

Reasons to roll over your lump-sum pension into an IRA account include the following:

1. Monthly payments from pensions do not keep pace with inflation. In other words, they do not have a cost–of–living adjustment as Social Security does. In 1980, $1,700 had the purchasing power of $4,029 by today's standards.[2] Imagine taking a monthly cut in pay from $4,029 to $1,700; that's the effect of inflation. Due to inflation, monthly pension checks received late in retirement don't look nearly as attractive as they may have initially appeared. If you rollover to an IRA, you have a chance to at least keep pace with inflation.

2. The monthly pension benefit can't be adjusted to provide lump sums for emergency situations. "When would I need a lump sum?" you might ask. Well, medical emergencies like organ transplants might require a large amount of money. Once pension funds are rolled over to an IRA, they can be accessed to provide lump sums in the event of an emergency.

3. Systematic monthly pension payments are taxable, and if you don't need monthly income from the pension, you'll incur unnecessary taxation. Leaving the money in an IRA to continue growing tax-deferred makes the most sense taxwise, especially if additional income is not needed.

4. If a monthly pension distribution is selected, and the pension recipient and the surviving spouse die soon after retirement, their heirs get nothing—not a dime. If your total lump sum pension was worth $300,000 dollars, and

---

2. Based upon an assumed 3 percent annual inflation rate.

you and your spouse received only a couple of payments before dying, your children or a charity will have missed out on a lot of money. Only the pension plan benefits from premature deaths. On the other hand, if you were to roll over the lump sum to an IRA, your heirs would receive 100 percent of that IRA balance.

Lump-sum rollovers can be valuable assets that, if properly managed, create a lifetime of income and a potential lump-sum benefit to the retiree's heirs. It is important to note that pension plan funds must be rolled directly to an IRA, or a 20 percent withholding tax will be deducted from the distribution, and the *entire* distribution becomes taxable. That's a fatal tax mistake! So rather than attempting to rollover to an IRA yourself, find a qualified financial professional to rollover and manage these funds for you.

The Pension Dilemma

If the pension plan does not allow for lump-sum rollovers to an IRA, or if the retiree for some reason simply elects to take a monthly income from the pension, decisions still have to be made to provide for a surviving spouse and to maximize the monthly income received.

Pension Plan
Survivor Benefits

If you select survivor benefits, your monthly payment will be lower to compensate the pension plan for the potentially longer period of time that payments will be made to you and your surviving spouse (as opposed to paying for the retiree's lifetime only). You'll be able to choose among options for the percentage of monthly payments that will continue for your surviving spouse, and the corresponding amount by which your monthly benefit will be reduced to make up for the spousal benefit. Survivor benefit elections are irrevocable; once made, they cannot be changed.

For example, Fred has worked for the phone company for thirty years and looks forward to his $3,000 monthly pension payment. However, he learns this $3,000 would be paid only to Fred during his lifetime; upon his death, his wife, Betty, would receive nothing. Fred investigates various survivor pension choices. He and Betty realize that she will need as much money as possible when Fred dies, especially given the fact that their family Social Security revenue will be reduced when Fred dies, and given that pension payments don't provide cost-of-living adjustments to keep up with inflation. Because of this, Fred and Betty consider the *joint and 100 percent survivor* benefit option. This option would reduce their monthly income, but would then continue to pay 100 percent of that reduced income to Betty upon Fred's death.

As you can see in fig. 5.1, this option would reduce Fred's monthly income from $3,000 to $2,100, but the $2,100 monthly payment would continue to Betty for the rest of her life. At first glance, this seems like the only sensible thing to do. After all, Fred can't just leave Betty with nothing when he dies.

COMPARISON OF PENSION BENEFITS WITH AND WITHOUT A SURVIVOR BENEFIT			
Pension Option Taken	Monthly Payment During Life	At Worker's Death, Spouse Receives	Cost to Worker in Lost Pension Benefits
Life Only Worker receives maximum lifetime benefit/spouse receives nothing after worker's death	$3,000 before taxes	$0 before taxes	Monthly - $0 Annually - $0 20 Years - $0
Joint & 50% Survivor Worker receives a lower lifetime benefit/spouse receives 50% of benefit after worker's death	$2,400 before taxes	$1,200 before taxes	Monthly - $600 Annually - $7,200 20 Years - $144,000
Joint & 100% Survivor Worker receives significantly lower lifetime benefit/spouse receives 100% of benefit after worker's death	$2,100 before taxes	$2,100 before taxes	Monthly - $900 Annually - $10,800 20 Years - $216,000

fig. 5.1
Source: Data from ING Financial & Investment, 2004.

Upon further investigation, however, Fred and Betty realize that, by electing the joint and 100 percent survivor benefit, they would essentially be buying a very expensive life insurance policy for $900 a month, which would only pay a benefit if Fred died before Betty. Furthermore, it wouldn't pay a lump sum of money, only the non-inflation-adjusted income of $2,100 for the balance of Betty's life. Additionally, if Betty died before Fred, he'd continue to receive the reduced $2,100 a month for the rest of his life, even though his survivor benefits would never be paid out. The $900 cut in pay could potentially turn out to be a gigantic waste of money.

There are several things you should carefully consider before deciding to take a reduced pension benefit:

- If your spouse predeceases you, then you will have reduced your own benefit for life with no benefit for you or your heirs.

- If you both live a full life and die within a year or two of each other (which is not unusual) little benefit, if any, will be realized after twenty to thirty years of reduced pension income.

- Your children will never inherit any benefits.

Obviously, the surviving spouse has to be taken care of. But the question remains: How should the surviving spouse be covered if the pension recipient dies first? Is there a better option? Yes, there is. The answer in many cases is pension maximization, a strategy that includes a life insurance policy, which may provide superior benefits and alternatives than the "joint and 100 percent survivor" pension options provided by the pension plan.

Pension Maximization

A permanent, individually owned life insurance policy is the economic workhorse behind the pension maximization option. Simply stated, using an individually purchased life insurance policy to provide the surviving spouse with replacement income can be less expensive than the significant reduction in monthly pension benefits incurred by the survivor option.

Fred is sixty-five and, if in good health, a guaranteed premium universal life policy for the amount of $500,000 on Fred's life would cost about $783 per month, which is certainly less than the $900 cut in pay incurred by the joint and 100 percent survivor option. If Fred had planned ahead and purchased the life insurance policy at age fifty-five instead of sixty-five, the monthly insurance premium would be $448 monthly. If Fred dies when Betty is sixty-five, she could buy an immediate annuity for $500,000, guaranteeing her a $3,000 monthly income for the balance of her life. If Fred dies when Betty is seventy-five, she'll only need $369,372 to purchase an immediate annuity that would provide $3,000 of monthly guaranteed income.[3] If Fred lives to normal life expectancy and dies at the age of 85, Betty could easily live off of the $500,000 insurance death benefit. The balance of the $500,000 life insurance proceeds at Betty's death can go to family or charity.

To determine whether pension maximization is right for you, you should consider the following points:

- When the worker dies, the pension will be replaced with income from the life insurance.

- If the spouse predeceases the worker, the worker will maintain the higher pension payment and will have the option

---

3. Immediate Fixed Annuities are long-term investments designed for retirement purposes. Generally, a portion of each annuity payment is a tax-free return of your investment in the contract and the remaining portion is taxable as ordinary income. Once your investment in the contract has been fully recovered, the full amount of each annuity payment is subject to tax as ordinary income. If you are under age fifty-nine and one-half, a 10 percent tax penalty may also apply. All guarantees are based on the claims-paying ability of the insurer.

to cash in or sell the life insurance policy, or to keep it for his family or a charity.

- If both spouses live long lives, monthly income is increased, because insurance costs are less than the monthly pension reduction for the joint and 100 percent survivor option.
- If the worker and spouse die simultaneously, then life insurance benefits can be passed on to the beneficiaries.

Does pension maximization always work? The resounding answer is no. Every pension plan is unique and charges different amounts for survivorship benefits, and each retiree's situation must be closely scrutinized to squeeze as much as possible from the pension. If, as in our example, Fred and Betty's monthly income would have been reduced by $450 rather than $900 monthly for the joint and 100 percent survivor benefit, then it would probably be better to forget about the insurance program and take the reduced joint and 100 percent survivor pension.

Additionally, if health issues make the cost of purchasing life insurance for Fred prohibitive, the pension maximization program won't work. Ideally, to reduce the insurance cost, the employee should purchase a permanent life insurance policy at as young an age as possible. The decision to purchase insurance and use the pension maximization program versus the traditional pension survivor benefit is really a simple math problem. But the numbers should be closely scrutinized before making this all-important financial decision. When the pension maximization program does fit the situation, it can provide extra monthly income and a lump-sum death benefit for your spouse and heirs, which is not available with the survivor benefit option of a pension plan.

Pension Maximization: Don and Jan

Don was a sixty-five–year-old university professor in excellent health who played racquetball on a regular basis. Jan, his sixty-three-year-old wife, was severely diabetic and had heart disease. While Don was lucky enough to have a pension, the university did not offer lump-sum rollovers; it only offered monthly income options. Don could choose between various survivor options in his pension plan, but two seemed to make the most sense given his situation. Don could receive monthly payments of $4,300 during his lifetime with no pension benefit for Jan at his death, or he could receive a reduced 100 percent joint and survivor benefit of $3,590, which Jan would continue to receive after Don's death.

Given Jan's shorter life expectancy, the couple elected to take the maximum benefit for Don. Being conservative, they still considered the possibility of Don dying first, and decided to purchase a $500,000 twenty-year-term life insurance policy on Don. The cost of this policy, $511 per month, was $200 per month less expensive than the cost of the survivor benefit option. Should Jan die first, this insurance could be canceled or kept for Don and Jan's children. Either way, Don retains his higher pension plan benefit for the balance of his life.

It is important to note that if the health roles were reversed and Don was sick (and therefore uninsurable) and Jan were healthy, they would be wise to elect the 100 percent joint and survivor benefit, which would provide the maximum benefit for Jan, the surviving spouse. It's also important to note that usually, purchasing a guaranteed premium universal life insurance policy in addition to a pension maximization plan is meant to ensure that the insurance wouldn't expire while the insured is still living. In this case, though, Jan had a short life expectancy, and a twenty-year-term life policy was was deemed to be sufficient.

Pension decisions are generally irrevocable, so there is no room for mistakes. If you decide to use a pension maximization plan, you must make sure of three things:

1. Make sure you're insurable. In other words, don't discard the joint and survivor benefit on the pension plan before determining eligibility and cost of permanent life insurance.

2. Make sure you purchase an insurance policy from a top-rated company (one that will be there in twenty-five to thirty years when the pension participant dies).

3. Make sure your spouse won't lose medical coverage after your death if you *don't* select the joint and survivor option. Some pension plans require the surviving spouse to have a continued affiliation with the company (such as a survivor benefit) in order to retain medical benefits under the company plan.

Know Your Pension Plan

There are things you need to know about your pension plan prior to retiring:

- How much will you receive?
- When will you become vested in the plan?
- What does the company consider the normal retirement age? (the age when you receive full benefits.)
- Will the plan allow lump sum distributions or only monthly payments?
- What will be your Social Security benefit? Will it be deducted from your pension benefit?
- Have you and your spouse declined in writing any pre-retirement survivor option? (This would pay benefits to your spouse even if you died prior to retirement.)

– What is the financial strength of your company's pension plan? Will the plan be able to meet future financial obligations?

Pension Guarantees

In 1999, 78 percent of S&P 500 companies had sufficient reserves to meet future pension payment obligations or were considered "overfunded." In 2007 only 36 percent of these same pension plans were considered to be capable of meeting future pension obligations.[4] Today, that number is even less due to the market declines of 2008 and early 2009. The annual report provided by your employer can give you the details of your particular pension.

There is, however, a government program that provides limited protection to the millions of American workers and retirees who are now or soon will be receiving pension payments. The Pension Benefit Guaranty Corporation (PBGC) guarantees pensions, just as the Federal Deposit Insurance Corporation (FDIC) guarantees deposits in a bank. If a bank becomes insolvent, each of its deposits is protected by the FDIC up to one hundred thousand dollars (in normal years).[5] If a pension plan becomes insolvent, the PBGC guarantees limited monthly pension payments depending on your age at retirement and the survivorship option you selected.

Don't think, however, that because of the PBGC, all is well; guarantee limits are restrictive. I know an individual who worked for thirty years in the auto industry before retiring at age fifty. Because he chose to retire at such a young age, his monthly pension payment will be cut by 65 percent if his ex-employer and its pension plan declare bankruptcy.

---

4. J.P. Morgan Asset Management, "Asset Class: Corporate DB Plans and Endowments," *Market Insight Series*, 2008, 44.

5. Currently, due to the recession and the financial crisis, the FDIC-insured rate has been increased to $250,000 through December 31, 2013.

For more information regarding the PBGC, see the resources page at the end of the book.

Conclusion

Like every retirement income source, pensions need to be understood, and you should carefully consider all means and sources of income to maximize the benefit for you and your spouse. Regardless of situation, those with a pension can greatly benefit from including pension funds into the overall retirement income plan. Properly planned, benefits from the pension plan can make a significant difference in the viability and longevity of a retirement income plan.

CHAPTER 6

WORKING DURING RETIREMENT

After Social Security and pension plans comes a third source of retirement income: work. Early in my career, I thought, like many people, that I would work until I could afford to retire and that retirement would take place as quickly as possible. But then an event happened that helped me to look at retirement differently.

I've always loved to fish, and I always wanted to see Alaska, so I booked an Alaskan fishing vacation for myself (yes, I have a very understanding wife). Upon arrival at the lodge, I was paired up with three retired men for five days of fishing. One of the men was a semiretired dentist named Ken who still saw patients one or two days a week. My other two fishing companions had both been successful businessmen before fully retiring. After fishing with these men for five days, I discovered something interesting: the two wealthy businessmen were actually jealous of Ken, not because he was wealthier—he wasn't—but because he had something meaningful to do. He was staying somewhat active in his profession, rather than fully retiring right away.

On that trip, I learned that retirement is not necessarily a state of being. It's a state of mind. And for many people, especially those of us who identify with our careers, it is difficult to move fully into retirement in one big step. This attitude has become a part of mainstream America as of late, with retirees either returning to the workforce or delaying retirement until much later than previous generations did.

Work and retirement used to be mutually exclusive: when the first ended, the second began. In fact, the dictionary defines *retirement* as "1. withdrawal from one's position or occupation or from active working life 2. a place of seclusion or privacy."[1] This definition certainly implies that when one retires, one withdraws from society and does not return. Today, however, a new trend is beginning to emerge that suggests work and retirement can easily coexist. As many as 50 percent of retirees return to the workforce to pursue a hobby job, a part-time career, or meaningful work that benefits others. Whatever the reason, working during retirement can provide fulfillment and another valuable source of income.

Reasons for Working Longer

There are many reasons why retirees may want to return to the workforce, perhaps to positions different from the ones they previously held. For example, some retirees like the idea of working in a more meaningful position that can add purpose to their lives and the lives of others. Others are looking to add to their assets or delay taking their Social Security by taking on a part-time or full-time position in an area they're interested in. Others are just looking to shift more gradually into full retirement by either cutting back their hours at their current job or finding a low-stress, part-time position elsewhere. Retirement today is becoming a gradual process rather than an abrupt cessation of work.

1. *Merriam-Webster Online Dictionary*, s.v. "Retirement"," http://www.merriam-webster.com/dictionary/retirement (accessed February 3, 2010).

Looking for Meaning

Many retirees begin retirement thinking that relaxation and leisure will be enough to fulfill their needs, only to find that the days seem endless and lacking in purpose. I observed this from my fishing partners. Some people find purpose in hobbies, and returning to work is not something they need to do; others' identities are tied to working, and they can get the sense of purpose they're looking for by either staying in their current position or finding a new, less stressful, retirement job.

According to a MetLife study[2] titled "Living Longer, Working Longer," a major motivation among retirees who returned to work was the quest for meaning; indeed, respondents' top reasons for working were "trying something different" or "contributing to society." This study found that retirement for today's retirees is more of a state of mind than a particular date; as long as there's some time for relaxation and freedom from the demands of a stressful job, retirees can feel as though they're retired, even if they're still working.

Perception of Old Age

Another variable to consider is that many retirees do not feel old enough to retire. According to the International Longevity Center[3], the majority of Americans do not believe that their chronological age reflects their "real" age, or how old they feel. They cite overall health, not a number, as the true determinant of age. Many who reach retirement age are healthy and can easily work a few more years before work-related stress becomes unmanageable and health starts to decline. Many new retirees are finding that they don't necessarily need the rest and leisure of full-time retirement.

---

2. David Delong, *Living Longer, Working Longer: The Changing Landscape of the Aging Workforce,* MetLife Mature Market Institute, Brochure, 2006, 6
3. Ibid.

Social Interaction

Some retirees find that the social aspect of work keeps them feeling healthy and makes them feel like vital members of society. Indeed, social interactions with coworkers can be more important than extra income to the overall well-being of some individuals. Such interpersonal connections might keep some retirees healthier longer. Staying mentally, physically, and socially engaged could lead to a more satisfying retirement experience.

Life Expectancy

It is likely that retirees today will live a very long time—much longer than they expect. It is important to realize this and work longer, if necessary, to secure the assets needed to fund a lengthy retirement. Imagine living thirty years into retirement and running out of assets after twenty years; this leaves ten years of unfunded retirement. It's tough to enjoy the "golden years" while surviving solely on Social Security.

If you haven't considered the length of your retirement, you may not have realized that roughly thirty years of leisure and rest may become boring over time. A good question to consider is whether five extra years of employment will cut into retirement leisure time too much. In most cases, the answer is no. A part-time position is a great way to break up monotony while bolstering retirement finances and adding value to the retirement years.

Working During Retirement: Richard and Beverly

During Richard's working life, he owned three auto dealerships. When he sold his dealerships, he had all the money he needed for life, and he was able to retire with a prospect of a comfortable future ahead of him. Shortly after his retirement, however, Beverly came home from shopping to find that Richard had completely reorganized her kitchen. Richard had even lined up the spices alphabetically. That was the final straw. Beverly insisted that Richard find something to do. Richard, recognizing that he missed the social interactions he had before retirement, decided that Beverly was right.

He did find something to do. He now drives a shuttle bus for a local ski resort in the winter and is a golf marshal in the summer. He gets free golfing and skiing, and in Richard's words, "They even pay me!" Both Richard and Beverly are enjoying their new retirement arrangement.

Calculating the Financial Impact of Working During Retirement

Some retirees have not saved enough for retirement. Others have saved diligently, but haven't properly managed their investments or have suffered investment losses during the past decade. Creating a thirty year stream of income requires a lot more money than most people realize, and many retirees are unprepared for the financial realities of retirement. What they fail to recognize is that they probably haven't adequately accounted for inflation, rising medical costs, or the possibility of long-term care. Medical costs in particular can have a substantial impact upon retirement assets. Few people understand how much a decision to continue working into retirement can contribute to their future financial security.

According to the Urban Institute[4], continuing to work into retirement can boost annual retirement income by an average of 9 percent per extra year worked. In some cases, money earned from even part-time retirement jobs may be enough to cover unforeseen

---

4. The Urban Institute, *Work and Retirement*, http://www.urban.org/toolkit /issues/socialsecurity.cfm.

expenses, allowing retirees to leave their retirement accounts untouched. If you don't have to draw from your retirement account, you can continue to take advantage of compounding interest and the growth potential of your investments. This will provide a greater future income and allow for a more comfortable retirement.

Improve Monthly Social Security Payments

As I discussed in the chapters on Social Security, delaying the start of Social Security payments can have a profound effect on monthly income and the total lifetime benefit. A retirement job can help retirees delay the start of Social Security by providing them with enough current income to cover day-to-day expenses.

Furthermore, Social Security payments are based on the top thirty-five years of earnings, and, in some cases, retirees do not have a full thirty-five years of earnings. Working during retirement can fill in gaps in your earnings record, increasing your Social Security paycheck once you claim the benefits.

Medical Expenses

Since most retirement jobs don't provide medical benefits, working past retirement can be an important way to pay for insurance coverage until the age of sixty-five, when Medicare starts. It's important to note that many retirees are unprepared for the often prohibitive costs of health insurance in the gap between retirement and the start of Medicare; furthermore Medicare also only covers a portion of medical expenses. Indeed, if employers offer medical benefits, they may be better than the benefits provided by Medicare.

Additionally, if you enjoy your current job and it offers medical benefits, it may be a good idea to continue in your current position rather than downsizing to a part-time position. Remaining at work until you can receive Medicare eliminates the need to pay expensive health insurance premiums. This allows money to stay in retirement accounts in order to accumulate interest.

How Much Longer Should I Work?

In the past, spouses had a tendency to retire at the same time in order to spend more time together during retirement. This meant wives who were younger than their husbands often retired early, if they had full-time careers at all. Today, couples still like to retire at the same time but more wives have careers, so many husbands work longer in order to retire at the same time as their generally younger wives. This has accounted for a roughly 9 percent increase in married men in the workforce in their mid to late sixties. Not only does this allow couples to enjoy their retirement years together, but it also provides a larger nest egg once they do retire and start living off of their retirement accounts.

Typically, Americans retire between ages sixty and sixty-four. For some, this is a fine time to retire. Others need to work a few more years in order to provide a better retirement. According to Alicia Munnell[5], the director of the Center for Retirement Research at Boston College, it's best to continue working until age sixty-six. This is generally the full retirement age for baby boomers, according to the U.S. Social Security Administration[6]. Others claim that working until seventy, when the maximum amount of Social Security can be claimed, is best, especially if health is good. The number of households adequately prepared for retirement would double if the baby boomers currently retiring between ages fifty-four and sixty-three delayed retirement until ages sixty-five to seventy.

If you plan to work past the traditional retirement age, it is important to let your boss know that you want to continue working for at least several years. Many bosses assume that older workers

---

5. Emily Brandon, *U.S. News & World Report*, "How Much Longer Will Boomers Need to Work?" August 11, 2008, http://www.usnews.com/money/personal-finance/retirement/articles/2008/08/11/how-much-longer-will-boomers-need-to-work.html.

6. Social Security Administration, *Full Retirement Age,* http://www.socialsecurity.gov/retire2/retirechart.htm.

are likely to retire within a year or two, so they pass them up for promotions or raises. Some employers begin to make such assumptions when their employees are as young as fifty-five, unaware some of their preretirees wish to continue working for up to fifteen additional years. Don't let yourself fall through the cracks.

Old Careers vs. New Careers

Often, working after retirement means you can pursue a new path. Many retirees who return to work do so in a field completely unrelated to their previous jobs. Baby boomer retirees today are more educated than past generations, with skills that can be used in many different careers. In fact, many employers today are looking to recruit older workers because (1) they know that there will be a shortage of labor once the majority of baby boomers have retired, and (2) older workers tend to have more experience than younger workers and can be transitioned into new positions easily. This allows retirees to pursue wholly new career paths that might bring them more satisfaction than did their previous careers. Retirement is a great time to try new things, especially if the goal of working after retirement is to learn a new skill or find a new area of enjoyment, rather than solely providing income.

A New Kind of Retirement: Len and Barbara

While on vacation with my family in Bryce Canyon National Park in Utah, I experienced tire trouble, which led me to meet two very interesting people who managed the local tire store.

Len and Barbara lived in the Midwest and enjoyed traveling the country in their motor home. After losing a close friend in the events of 9/11, they decided that life was too uncertain to put off their dreams of traveling any longer.

They retired from their jobs, sold their home, gave away any belongings that could not fit in their motor home, and became full-time RVers.

As full time RVers, Len and Barbara have traveled the country, occasionally stopping and working when they get tired of the road. Since retiring, they have managed a pool-cleaning business in New York, sold admission tickets to an amusement park in North Carolina, and operated an RV park in Texas. For the last three years, they have been running the tire shop at Bryce Canyon, but they assure me that if they get bored, they will be moving on to something new.

Len and Barbara's children and siblings are spread across the nation, so they take time off work occasionally for a road trip to visit family. Apparently, there are several million retirees in the United States who choose to live this way. Various organizations like Good Sam RV Club support the full-time RVer lifestyle.

The AARP conducted a study[7] that compared how new retirement jobs stack up compared to older jobs, regarding compensation, stress, and flexibility. While the study showed that even though wages are substantially lower in new careers and that nearly one-quarter of career-changers lose health insurance coverage, it also found that the majority of retirees enjoy their new job more than their previous job, even if the new one is substantially less prestigious.[8] This is most likely due to the fact that most retirees place a high value on their time and want to escape a nine-to-five

7. Richard Johnson, Janette Kawachi, and Eric Lewis, "Older Workers on the Move: Recareering in Later Life," *The Urban Institute*, 2009, http://www.urban.org/url.cfm?ID=1001272.

8. Ibid.

position, rather than wanting to escape the workforce altogether. According to the AARP study, pursuing new careers, or "recareering," is common for retirees.

Recareering Opportunity: Glen and Vickie

At the age of fifty-four, Glen owned a successful car repair shop and Vickie, fifty-three, was an emergency room nurse. They shared a love for golfing, and both had been saving toward a (hopefully) golf-filled retirement.

One day, I received a phone call from Glen informing me that he and Vickie had decided to retire immediately. I ran through the numbers and told him that wasn't possible with the amount of money they had saved—they needed another ten years or so of employment to meet their goals.

But as it turned out, retirement had a very different meaning to them than it did to me. To them, it meant moving onto different things. They moved to Mesquite, Nevada, where Glen now repairs golf carts instead of cars a couple of days each week, while Vickie works in the golf shop. With income from the sale of his repair shop and the wages they receive, they're earning about the same amount of money as before they "retired." They golf every day, and they love their retirement!

Another way to make work more enjoyable is to develop new skills that can either prepare you for more responsibility in a current job or provide the qualifications necessary for a new job. By keeping your skills up-to-date, you'll make yourself more valuable to companies. Retirement is long enough that you even might consider returning to school to learn a new profession. Some colleges offer free or discounted classes for retirees, and since an entirely new degree is not usually necessary for a small career change, a few classes may be all you need. Returning to school can help retirees increase their odds of finding a job that they enjoy, which can make the last few years of work far more enjoyable than a standard nine-to-five job.

Warning: Working During Retirement isn't Always Possible

Planning to work during retirement should not be an excuse for lack of financial preparation. In the keynote address of the Retirement Income Symposium in October of 2009, Dan Houston, head of the retirement and investment services division of Principal Financial Group, presented some "brutal facts" about the lack of financial preparations of those soon retiring. Houston cited studies that found that, although 72 percent of workers said they planned to work in retirement, at least half of all retirees cannot work, either because they do not have the right skillsets or are not healthy enough to work, or because they are prevented from working by their spouses' health.[9]

Working beyond the normal retirement age or finding supplemental work during retirement might be an optimal plan, but it is a plan that cannot be depended upon. Therefore, you still must do all you can to prepare and save for retirement during your working years.

A Concluding Note

The baby boomer retirement will not necessarily be a cessation of work; it's just a change of pace. Retirement is doing the things you want to do, not necessarily ceasing all activity. Some people quit their full-time positions to pursue hobbies that can provide income, such as working at a golf course, painting, or working at a

9. James J. Green, "Solutions for the New Retirement Reality," *Investment Advisor*, 2009, http://www.investmentadvisor.com/Issues/2009/December-2009/Pages/Solutions-for-the-New-Retirement-Reality.aspx.

marina. Some people simply want a lower-key, part-time position at a bookstore or a retail store so that they remain active, while still having time for leisure and relaxation. Others simply need something to do other than staying home all day. Whatever the reason, the face of retirement is shifting to include new opportunities and pursuits for retirees.

CHAPTER 7

REVERSE MORTGAGES

Income from Social Security, pensions, and even post-retirement employment can help you build a worry-free and satisfying retirement. Income from your home might also add to your retirement income stream. In my opinion, an ideal retirement includes a home that is free and clear of any type of mortgage. **I further believe that home equity should only be accessed for absolutely necessary income and lifestyle needs. The equity in your home should never be used for investment speculation or, for that matter, even for "safe" investments.**

However, for various reasons, some retirees find themselves cash-strapped, and a reverse mortgage may provide lifestyle-saving retirement income solutions. Many retirees find themselves living on a limited fixed income while either owning their home free and clear or owing little money on the mortgage. In times past, the only way these house-rich, cash-poor people could remedy this situation was to sell the house or take out a home equity loan. Home equity loans require monthly repayments and only add to cash flow problems. Beginning in the 1960s, however, a new tool was introduced for retirees in this situation: the reverse mortgage.

In a nutshell, a reverse mortgage allows house-rich individuals to tap the equity in their home and make their house pay them, rather than the other way around. It is essentially a loan against a home. While a regular mortgage decreases the mortgage balance and increases home equity over time, a reverse mortgage works in the opposite direction; instead of the homeowner paying the lender, the lender pays the homeowner. Over time, the mortgage loan balance increases and the equity decreases, because the equity in the house is what is being used to finance the payments to the homeowner.

Many retirees would prefer to grow old in their homes, but they also have a need for cash during retirement. A reverse mortgage allows them not only to keep their home, but also to receive payments, or a lump sum if they choose, from the home equity. Even more appealing, there are no payments due on the reverse mortgage until the homeowners sell the home, permanently move out of the home ("permanently" is usually defined by lenders as one year or more), or die. While some look upon this feature favorably, others worry that their children will be stuck with a large debt after they die. This *cannot* happen. The lender can only look to the value of the home for repayment, regardless of the amount of money owed. In other words, the children won't be left with debt.

Reverse mortgages are not for everyone, but neither are they a scam, as some perceive them to be. My hope is that the information in this chapter will shed some light on the advantages and disadvantages of reverse mortgages, so that you can decide whether this is a viable option for you.

Three essential facts to keep in mind while considering reverse mortgages are:

1. You or your children cannot owe more than the value of the home.

2. You retain title to the property—in other words, you can't be kicked out of your home.

3. You receive payments instead of making them.

If the circumstances are right, a reverse mortgage can be a useful and intelligent option to supplement retirement income.

Eligibility

A reverse mortgage is only available to seniors age sixty-two and older who either own their home or owe little enough that the balance can be paid off by the reverse mortgage (usually 50 percent or less of the home's appraised value). Only the principal residence in which the homeowner resides is eligible; second homes and apartments are generally not eligible for a reverse mortgage. Any other debt against the home, such as a home equity loan, must be paid off prior to, or when receiving, a reverse mortgage. Furthermore, only single-family dwellings are eligible for reverse mortgages.

An important benefit of a reverse mortgage is that there are no income requirements for qualification, because there are no payments due until the homeowners either sell the property or die, at which time the balance of the reverse mortgage, plus accrued interest, is due. The reverse mortgage can be paid off by heirs selling the home or through refinancing. If, by chance, the reverse mortgage loan is larger than the home's value at the homeowner's death, the lender simply takes over the home. The estate of the homeowner and the homeowner's children will owe nothing. This is because reverse mortgages are nonrecourse loans, meaning the lender can only look to the value of the house for repayment, not to the homeowner or the homeowner's children.

Advantages of Reverse Mortgages

Reverse mortgages, like any loans, have both pros and cons that should be considered carefully when you're deciding whether or not to take one out. The main advantage of a reverse mortgage is that it is a flexible financial planning product, since there are very few, if any, restrictions on how the money can be spent. But there are many other advantages to take into account as well.

Extra Money for Expenses

One obvious benefit of a reverse mortgage is additional monthly income. This income can be used to wipe out debts such as auto loans and outstanding credit card balances. In many instances, money received from the reverse mortgage loan is used to pay off the existing mortgage, thus ending the monthly mortgage payment obligation.

Maintain Independence

For some, a reverse mortgage makes the difference between maintaining independence and depending upon others. Making improvements or modifications to a home to maintain it as a livable residence or paying for in-home health care can help retirees avoid moving to an apartment or assisted living facility. In a similar vein, reverse mortgage proceeds can be put away to meet future needs, such as long-term care or unforeseen medical expenses.

Reverse Mortgage for Income: Anthony and Lisa

Anthony was in good health at the age of eighty-two, while his wife, Lisa, was seventy-six and in poor health. They lived in California, where Anthony worked as an engineer. During his career, he had accumulated an IRA worth $900,000, but through a series of bad investments and annual withdrawals of $30,000 to $50,000 over seventeen years, their once-healthy IRA had dwindled to about $200,000.

I first met Anthony and Lisa after they moved to Utah. They told me they needed a minimum income from their investments of $40,000 annually. I explained that there was no way to maintain that type of withdrawal schedule on a $200,000 account without running out of money in five or six years. Luckily, their home in Utah was paid off, with a value of around $500,000.

We discussed a plan that I included tapping into their home equity in five years, when their retirement account run out of money. This would allow them to continue taking income for at least six additional years, which might be sufficient to last their lifetime. Upon their deaths, their children could sell the house, pay back the Federal Housing Administrations reverse mortgage, and keep the remaining proceeds from the sale for themselves.

Retain Home Ownership

An advantage that many people don't think about when they weigh regular loans against reverse mortgages is that the borrower, not the bank, retains ownership of the home throughout the term of the loan. Furthermore, there is no risk of defaulting on the loan and having the house taken away by the lender, since there are no payments due until the house is either vacant for more than one year or the owner has died.

Tax-Free and Federally Insured Money

The money received from a reverse mortgage is tax-free, as well. Because the money paid to a borrower is considered a loan at the time of disbursement, there are no tax requirements on it, regardless of whether it is disbursed as a lump sum or as monthly payments. The loan is also federally insured if you use a Home Equity Conversion Mortgage (HECM) loan, so if the lender defaults, there will be no problem with payments to the borrower.

Eliminating the Existing Mortgage Payment

Reverse mortgages aren't just about receiving an extra monthly income. In many instances, reverse mortgages can eliminate existing mortgage payments. In those instances in which a mortgage payment is a significant drain on an overall retirement income plan, it is best to wipe out the monthly mortgage payment obligation with a reverse mortgage.

Eliminating this monthly payment leads to smaller withdrawals on retirement accounts, thus lengthening the time the retirement income plan can provide an ever-important stream of income to the retiree.

Reverse Mortgage to Alleviate a Mortgage Payment: Ralph and Elaine

Ralph, sixty-seven, and Elaine, sixty-five, had roughly $170,000 in mortgage debt from a first and second mortgage. Their house was appraised at $265,000, so they owed about 65 percent of the appraised value of the home.

Ralph, who worked in the construction business, has had little to no income over the past two years due to the economic downturn, and Elaine had health problems, creating large and ongoing medical expenses. As a result, Ralph's once-healthy 401(k) had diminished to nearly nothing over the years.

The monthly payment on their first and second mortgages amounted to $1,595. At their ages, at least 50 percent of the home would have to be paid off to qualify for a reverse mortgage. Because Ralph and Elaine owed 65 percent, it was unlikely that they would be eligible for a reverse mortgage.

Recently, however, Elaine received a small inheritance. Considering Elaine's health, I suggested that instead of investing the money, they should put the inheritance toward their mortgage, thus enabling them to qualify for a reverse mortgage.

They took out the reverse mortgage, which eliminated the $1,595 monthly mortgage burden. This now provides them with the extra money they need to pay their medical bills and enjoy a less stressful retirement.

Disadvantages of Reverse Mortgages

Reverse mortgages, despite the advantages described above, are not for everyone. Certain retirees who either don't need the money or are using government assistance will need to consider carefully whether a reverse mortgage will help or hinder their financial situation.

Closing Costs

In the past the biggest disadvantage of a reverse mortgage were the closing costs. They were generally much higher than regular home equity loans; often twice the closing costs of a traditional mortgage. In a very recent development, we have seen large reverse mortgage providers slash their closing costs to make reverse mortgage fees fall in line with the costs of a traditional mortgage. Hopefully the trend will catch on industry-wide, making reverse mortgages more affordable.

Because of closing costs, a reverse mortgage is not a good short-term option; it only makes sense if the disadvantages of the closing costs are outweighed by the advantages of freeing up monthly income. If you plan to move in the near future, dollars spent on closing costs would be wasted money. You should really only consider a reverse mortgage if you plan to stay in the house for at least seven to ten years past the loan origination date.

Extra Insurance Required

Borrowers are required to carry insurance for the life of the loan in order to protect the lender from losing money if the home's value

SCOTT M. PETERSON, ChFC

falls. Borrowers continue to be responsible for real estate taxes, homeowners insurance, and home repairs.

Emotional Insecurity
Reverse mortgages may be emotionally draining for some borrowers with long-held, negative attitudes toward debt. Some people are uncomfortable about taking out any debt against a home, especially if that home is owned free and clear. This is something you should consider carefully. If the extra money is not worth the anxiety of accumulated debt each month, a reverse mortgage may not be the right option for you.

Reduced Legacy for Heirs
Retirees who wish to leave a legacy for their heirs may not like a reverse mortgage. Once you enter into a reverse mortgage, you use up a portion of your home's equity, so it can't be passed on to heirs. Heirs will only receive the excess money from the sale of the home, minus the amount of the reverse mortgage loan.

Effects on Low-Income Assistance
Those who are eligible for low-income assistance should investigate whether a reverse mortgage would disqualify them for that aid. Some programs, such as Medicaid, consider loan disbursements an asset, which means that certain Medicaid recipients may become ineligible after receiving reverse mortgage payments. Note, though, that Social Security and Medicare are not affected by reverse mortgage payments.

The Application Process
If you decide that a reverse mortgage is a good option, the next step is meeting with an approved reverse mortgage specialist to discuss eligibility, loan amount, and payment options. The older the applicant, the more the home equity becomes accessible, and the more money he or she can borrow. Amounts available to borrow will vary from lender to lender and borrower to borrower. The

80

maximum limit for 2011 is $625,500 in my area, but a reverse mortgage consultant can provide a more accurate figure for your individual situation and location.

Reverse mortgage payments can be either flexible or fixed, depending on your preferences. You can take a lump sum at the beginning of the loan, which is often used to pay off the existing mortgage. Alternatively, you can set up fixed monthly payments or set up available funds as a line of credit when needed, or use a combination of these methods. For example, you can take a lump sum to pay off your existing mortgage, then set up the remainder of the loan as a line of credit to be used for unexpected medical bills or other emergencies.

Once applicants talk to a reverse mortgage consultant, they are required to participate in an education session with a counselor approved by the U.S. Department of Housing and Urban Development. Family members and children are invited to attend as well, since they'll be responsible for selling the home or refinancing the loan when the homeowner dies. The session covers the legal and financial obligations of a reverse mortgage, as well as alternatives to a reverse mortgage, to make sure it is the right decision for the retiree.

After the education session, the reverse mortgage consultant will help the applicant fill out the paperwork and provide a disclosure outlining the total estimated loan cost. An appraisal of the home's value will be required to determine the amount of the loan. Title or mortgage insurance must also be purchased to protect the lender from the risk of losing money when the house is sold, either because of declining home values or claims against the ownership of the property.

After you're approved, you'll go through underwriting and closing. Closing is generally conducted in your home. Before closing, you must agree upon all closing costs with the reverse mortgage lender, select methods of payments, and provide any applicable mortgage insurance documents. Once everything is agreed upon and closed, the documents are sent to you, and fund disbursements begin.

Is a Reverse Mortgage a Good Option for You?

A reverse mortgage offers a no-payment, no-default loan that can help you make ends meet or fulfill goals during retirement. If you meet eligibility requirements, and if you've weighed the pros and cons, the only question left to answer is whether or not a reverse mortgage is absolutely necessary for you.

Generally speaking, a reverse mortgage is not a good idea unless it's clear that your retirement finances are going to dry up before your retirement years are over. If you face this prospect, a reverse mortgage is a good option, especially when the only other options are borrowing money from your children or begrudgingly selling your home and downsizing to a less expensive home or apartment. That said, choosing among these alternatives often comes down to a matter of personal preference. Some homeowners prefer the emotional security of living in a house in which they spent their lives and watched their children grow up, so a reverse mortgage is worth it. On the other hand, some homeowners prize the financial security of a paid-off, debt-free home, so downsizing to a smaller home might be a better option.

Whatever you decide, a reverse mortgage should be considered carefully and researched thoroughly. If you decide to pursue one, you should factor the payments from the lender into your overall retirement income plan to improve the chances that the funds will cover any shortfalls. A retirement income planner can help you decide whether a reverse mortgage would be a viable option, help you locate a reverse mortgage specialist, and incorporate your reverse mortgage into your overall retirement income plan.

CHAPTER 8

MANAGING INVESTMENTS
DURING RETIREMENT

Now that I've discussed Social Security, pensions, working during retirement, and reverse mortgages, it's time to discuss the fifth and final significant source of retirement income: personal investments.

Every home has a junk drawer where random, unorganized items are kept. At my house, it's in the kitchen. If I'm ever in need of a paper clip, shoelace, pair of pliers, or a stapler, the first place I look is in the junk drawer. It's not that the items in the junk drawer don't have value—they do. It's just called a junk drawer because it's unorganized.

As someone who has managed retirement money for a quarter of a century, I find that helping a new retiree organize all the various and sundry investments they've collected over a working career is similar to organizing the old junk drawer. There's the whole life insurance policy Dad bought at your birth, the Roth IRA you contributed to for a couple of years and then left to grow, and of course the 401(k) you left at your ex-employer. Like the bits and pieces in the junk drawer, all of these items have value; the challenge is organizing and managing these assets, as well as more significant assets like lump-sum pension payments and 401(k) rollovers, into a stream of income that will last for decades.

Creating the Investment Management Plan

Just as there is no one-size-fits-all investment plan for every individual, there is no one-size-fits-all investment plan for every stage of an individual's life. Over time, the financial markets will change, as will your needs and goals; that's why you will need to periodically review your situation to keep your investment program on track.

The development of an investment management plan is highly personalized and involves answering a number of key questions:

- **Goals.** Why are you investing the money? Do you primarily need current income or growth? Is the money being set aside for future emergencies or to pass money onto your posterity?

- **Time horizon.** When will you need the money? Now? Ten years from now? Twenty years from now?

- **Liquidity.** How liquid or accessible does your money need to be?

- **Risks.** How tolerant are you of volatile markets? Have you made poor decisions during past market swings? Will you be tempted to do the same in the future?

- **Taxes.** How will investment gains add to your overall tax burden? How do you minimize taxation of investment gains?

- **Economic considerations.** What is the rate of inflation? What are the current interest rates? How is the overall economy doing?

Once you answer these key questions, you'll need to implement various strategies to reach your desired outcome. For most investors, following these strategies is overwhelming, which is why I highly recommend using a qualified financial professional to help you with an investment management plan that matches your retirement needs. These important strategies include:

- Investments in stocks as part of a *long-term* strategy
- Diversification
- The use of low or noncorrelated assets
- Asset allocation

Let's take a closer look at these strategies.

Investing in Stocks

Earlier in the book, I addressed the risks of inflation. Stocks are one of the few major asset classes that have been able to stay ahead of inflation over the long run. Some people fear stocks as "too risky," but a well-diversified portfolio of stocks invested for the *long term* is far less risky than the alternatives. Stocks will be more volatile in the short term than other types of investments, but they are a necessary component of a successful retirement income plan.[1]

Simply put, investing solely in "safe," low-yield, non-inflation-beating investments during retirement is financial suicide. Retirees who avoid stocks altogether may avoid the temporary anxiety of market volatility, but they condemn themselves to

---

1. The views expressed are those of the author and not a recommendation to buy or sell securities, or of any particular asset allocation strategy. These investment guidelines are not intended to represent investment advice that is appropriate for all investors. Each investor's portfolio must be constructed based on the individual's financial resources, investment goals, risk tolerance, investing time horizon, tax situation, and other relevant factors. Please discuss with your financial advisor before implementing an investment plan.

losing purchasing power day by day, until their once-healthy retirement account is so diminished by inflation that it can't meet their daily needs. Investing solely in bank accounts and certificates of deposit is the "safest" way I know to systematically lose purchasing power.

According to Ibbotson, if you had invested one dollar each in treasury bills, long-term government bonds, and large U.S. stocks in 1926, your values at the end of 2010 would be $21 in treasury bills, $93 in long-term government bonds, and $2,982 in large U.S. stocks. The value of those U.S. stocks would have been $3,246 in 2007, so the crash of 2008 obviously had a significant impact.[3] Still, I would gladly take the $2,982 invested in stocks versus the paltry sums of $21 or $93 realized from the "safe" investments in treasury bills and government bonds.[4]

The problem of people losing money in the stock markets lies with the investors, not the markets. Historical market research shows that negative and positive return cycles for the stock market can be as long as seventeen years. But according to a Dalbar study[5], the average holding period for investors in stock mutual funds is only about three years. No wonder the public is disillusioned with the stock market! That study may explain the average investor's severe chronic underperformance in comparison with stock market averages, as explained in chapter 1. Purchasing stocks for the short

2. Roger G. Ibbotson and Rex A. Sinquefield, *SBBI 2009 Yearbook: Market Results for 1926–2009: Stocks, Bonds, Bills, and Inflation (SBBI) Yearbook*, classic ed., (Chicago: Ibbotson Associates, 2009).

3. Roger G. Ibbotson and Rex A. Sinquefield, *SBBI 2007 Yearbook: Market Results for 1926–2007: Stocks, Bonds, Bills, and Inflation (SBBI) Yearbook*, classic ed., (Chicago: Ibbotson Associates, 2007).

4. The effects of taxes, fees, and transaction costs are not included. Assumes reinvestment of income. Past performance does not guarantee future results.

5. Dalbar Institute, *Quantitative Analysis of Investor Behavior: What Investors Really Do…and How to Counteract It*, Extract from the report *QAIB 2008*, Advisor ed., 2008: 7, http://www.scribd.com/doc/13096471/DALBAR-QAIB-2008.

term is reckless gambling; holding them for the long term is prudent investing.[6]

As the first decade of the new century ends, I often hear people say, "I haven't made money in a decade with stocks." For many, that statement is true, but most investors forget that the reason they have any money at all is because they were invested in stocks during the nineties, when the stock market was up over 400 percent. As Nick Murray says[7], "the stock market is the most efficient mechanism for transferring wealth from impatient people to patient people." Don't purchase stocks if you have less than a ten-year investment time horizon. If you want to keep up with inflation, purchase stocks and give them an appropriately long time to grow. Of course, every individual and portfolio is unique. All have different time horizons, risk tolerances, and growth and liquidity needs that will determine the percentage of stocks that should be included in a portfolio. With retirements lasting up to thirty years, stocks need to play a part in a successful retirement investment strategy.

Diversification

Most people understand the basic concept of diversification: don't put all of your eggs in one basket. The ancient Greeks understood that concept very well. Whenever they had a harvest of grain to ship to a faraway port, they would divide the grain into several different ships and send the ships by different trade routes or at different times of the year. This ensured that if a ship was lost at sea, an entire harvest wouldn't be lost as well. But even if you understand the concept of diversification, it's still easy to get caught in a trap.

6. U.S. stocks fluctuate in price so that value of an investment can go down depending on market conditions. Stock prices may fluctuate due to stock market volatility and market cycles, as well as circumstances specific to a company.
7. Nick Murray, *Behavioral Investment Counseling* (Southold, NY: Nick Murray Company, 2008), 83.

The biggest obstacle to diversification is retirees' tendency to hold on to large portions of company stock. I can recall numerous conversations over the course of my career with new retirees who became millionaires because they were given, and held onto, large amounts of company stocks. I heard the same argument from all of them. "What could possibly happen to my Citigroup, General Motors, or GE stock? These are the best-run companies in the world." But today, those individuals who diversified their retirement holdings out of a single company stock are doing much better than those who didn't.

In his book *Behavioral Investment Counseling*, Nick Murray advises adhering to a couple of rules to help you stay diversified as an investor:

1. "I will never own enough of any one thing to be able to make a killing in it."

2. "I will never own enough of any one thing to be able to get killed by it."[8]

Ultimately, the benefits of a diversified portfolio are reduced volatility and more competitive returns. Diversification means you probably won't be hitting the home runs that are possible with a concentrated portfolio, but you probably won't be striking out either. For the record, the goal of a diversified portfolio is to produce an inflation-adjusted return to last you a long time, not to speculate or roll the dice with your retirement funds.[9]

---

8. Ibid, 86.

9. Diversification may help reduce, but cannot eliminate, risk of investment losses. Historical performance relative to risk and return points to, but does not guarantee, the same relationship for future performance. There is no assurance that by assuming more risk, you are guaranteed to achieve better results.

Low or Noncorrelated Assets in a Diversified Portfolio
In the world of statistics, correlation refers to the strength of the linear relationship between two random variables. When two variables move exactly in sync with each other, they have a *perfect positive correlation,* or *+1 correlation;* when they move in exact opposition to each other, they have a *perfect negative correlation,* or *-1 correlation.* When there is a 50 percent chance of each variable moving in either direction at any time, they have *zero correlation.*

In the world of investments, correlation is the same. It's a statistical measure of how two investments move in relationship to each other, and it's often a part of advanced portfolio management (see fig. 8.1).

HOW CORRELATION WORKS

High correlation

Low correlation

These diagrams are for illustrative purposes only and do not represent the correlation of any actual securities or indexes.

fig. 8.1

One strategy to reduce volatility is to create portfolios that contain investments with low correlation.[10] For example, U.S. stocks and international bonds have a low correlation. Therefore, if the international bond portion of the portfolio drops, the U.S. stock portion of the portfolio is not likely to be affected, and vice versa. If an investment portfolio only consists of highly correlated investments (in other words, investment that move roughly in sync with each other), when market and economic conditions that effect that asset type worsen it is likely the entire portfolio will take a hit. Adding assets with low or zero correlation to your portfolio should help prevent this.

To give a simple example of correlation in a portfolio, imagine you own stock in separate companies that sell snow shovels, lawnmowers, and bread. The stocks of the snow shovel and lawnmower companies have a negative correlation: in the winter the snow shovel company does well, while the lawnmower company does poorly. The reverse is true in the summer; lawnmowers are in high demand, and snow shovels sell poorly. The stocks of the two companies move in almost perfect opposition to each other; their stock alternatively goes up and down in price as people buy their products. The season of the year drives sales, which affects the price of their stock. The bread company, on the other hand, would show a zero correlation with both the snow shovel and the lawnmower companies, because people will buy bread at any time of the year. Its stock will move completely independent from the lawnmower and

---

10. Noncorrelated investments cover a whole range of potential investments, including real estate, private equity, and commodities, along with alternative investment strategies which seek to generate positive returns irrespective of the direction of the market. Investing involves risk including loss of principal.

snow shovel companies'. Historically, commodities,[11] real estate[12], bonds, and stocks (both domestic and international) have exhibited a history of positive and negative correlation with each other.[13]

In the past, ensuring your portfolio included stocks with low correlation was easier—you could simply invest internationally. Today, given our increasingly global community, what happens in the U.S. has immediate impact on the rest of the world, and vice versa. In most cases, it's impossible to achieve a perfectly negative correlation, meaning that investments will never move in exact opposition to each other, but you can achieve a negatively correlated portfolio by diversifying your assets across various asset classes. Historically, a low-correlated investment portfolio will begin with investments in stocks and bonds. While stocks have earned more throughout history, bonds have moved somewhat independently of stocks, so investing in both offers a hedge against volatility in either market.

Historically, portfolios that are balanced by low correlation have performed better than those that are not, and have displayed less volatility.

---

11. Commodity based instruments are created to reflect, at any given time, the market price of the commodity owned by the instrument at that time less expenses and liabilities. The price received upon the sale of the shares, which trade a market price, may be more or less than the value of the commodity represented by them. Commodity markets have historically been extremely volatile, creating the potential for losses regardless of the length of time the shares are held. In addition, suspensions or disruptions of market trading in the commodities markets may adversely affect the value of your shares.

12. Real Estate investments involve investments that are subject to substantial risks including but not limited to: 1) the possibility that sale or redemption may be for more or less than the original amount invested, 2) the absence of a public market for these securities, 3) limited transferability and lack of liquidity, 4) the possibility of substantial delay in making distributions, 5) no assurance that the stated objectives will be met.

13. The risks associated with investing in International Equities include differences in regulation of financial data and reporting, currency exchange differences, as well as economic and political systems that may be different from those in the United States.

Asset Allocation

Academic research shows that asset allocation is by far the largest determining factor in investment portfolio returns, accounting for over 90 percent of the returns of a portfolio. Asset allocation is the process by which an individual spreads his or her investments over many categories with the goal of enhancing returns and meeting objectives with the lowest possible risk.

The study of asset allocation helps us to know that specific security selection (Exxon versus Coca-Cola stock) makes little difference in the performance of a portfolio as compared to choosing the right category of investment (stocks versus bonds). It is interesting to see so much energy exerted to find the "perfect stock" that will triple in value or find the "hot" mutual fund, when research has shown that all these efforts produce very little. In the long run, the specific investment you own may not matter as much as what category of investments you own.

The consensus among financial professionals is that asset allocation is one of the most important decisions that investors make, and can mean the difference between remaining financially self-sufficient or relying on children for support; between absorbing rising costs with confidence or losing financial freedom; and between generating income for a lifetime or outliving assets.

Combining Diversification, Noncorrelation, and Asset Allocation

Once you've answered the questions at the beginning of the chapter regarding investment goals, time horizon, liquidity needs, risk tolerance, taxes, and so on, your investment advisor should be able to put together a customized portfolio that incorporates the principles of diversification, noncorrelation, and asset allocation. Some investors with long time horizons and high risk tolerance should have a high percentage of their portfolios invested in stocks. On the other hand, investors with short-term liquidity needs and low risk tolerance can avoid the volatility of stocks altogether, and should put their money in less volatile, lower-yielding investments.

Investor Beware

The Media

It is important to remember that the media is in the business of selling advertising and that they accomplish this through viewership. Driving large numbers of people back to their product is the goal, whether it's a magazine, television program, newspaper, or even the nightly news. They are all in the business of selling something for a profit. Giving accurate, sound investment advice is not even on their radar screens. To catch people's attention and increase viewership, stories have to be exciting and extraordinary. At our office, we call the media hype "financial pornography."

For example, *Money* Magazine has never run a cover story about the Nobel-Prize-winning academic research on diversification and asset allocation. Although this information is important, it's boring. Instead, the cover of *Money Magazine* runs stories with headlines meant to grab attention: "The Hot Stocks to Buy Now!" or "The Mutual Funds You Need This Year!" or my personal favorite, which seems to work well for them after every market correction, "Where You Should Move Your Money Now!"[14]

Then, of course, cable news displays a twenty-four-hour–a-day analysis of the stock market, economy, valuation of the dollar, and the price of oil. Never does it share any academic research on proven investment strategies. *That* would be giving good advice, not selling products.

It is my belief that this daily barrage of information only confuses investors and leads them to believe that they (or their financial

---

14. Michael Sivy and Eric Garcia, "Where to Put Your Money," Money, August 1, 2004.

advisor) should consistently beat the markets by knowing when to jump in or out of them, or that their financial advisor should know how to find the hot but undiscovered stock that will make them instantly rich. Furthermore, I am concerned it may cloud the investor's ability to think through things and to match long-term historical perspectives with their own (possibly very long) life expectancy. Be careful with your investing. Stick with sound and principled investment strategies and avoid following the media hype.

Market Timing

Peter Lynch, the former manager of the Fidelity Magellan Fund, was quoted as saying, "Far more money has been lost by investors preparing for corrections or trying to anticipate corrections than has been lost in corrections themselves."[15] No one can reliably time the market; you'd have to know not only when to get out, but also when to get back in. The reality is that it is not the *timing* of the market that provides returns, but the *time spent in* the market. I am constantly amazed that the average investor somehow thinks he or she has a knack for market timing, when even the most educated and experienced professionals in the investment industry have proven that it can't be consistently accomplished.

From 1989 to 2008, the S&P 500 averaged an 8.4 percent return during the 5,049 trading days of that time period.[16] Missing only the ten best days would have reduced investment returns to 4.9 percent. Missing out on the fifty best days of the market, only one-tenth of 1 percent of trading days, would have transformed the 8.4 percent gain to a 2.8 percent loss![17]

15. Larry Swedroe, "The Smartest Things Ever Said about Market Timing," *CBS Money Watch*, Dec 25, 2009, http://moneywatch.bnet.com/investing/blog/wise-investing/the-smartest-things-ever-said-about-market-timing/1089/.
16. The S&P 500 stock index is a widely recognized, unmanaged index of common stocks. It is not possible to invest directly in an index.
17. Franklin Templeton Investments, *RetireMetrics: Build a Better Retirement,*

The appeal of market timing is obvious: avoiding periods of poor performance improves returns. However, timing the market consistently is extremely difficult. I have yet to find anyone who can do it. Many people are willing to take your money and try to exhibit their proficiency in timing the market, but remember: even a broken clock is right twice a day. Likewise, an unreliable money manager can occasionally be right, even if only by accident. Don't get caught up in the emotional roller coaster and waste money attempting to time the markets. I base my opinions on academic research and experience, not the ever-present "financial pornography" that attempts to persuade us otherwise.

Retirement is a time for methodical, proven investment strategies and lots of patience, not high-risk investing experiments, no matter how exciting they may seem at the moment. A thirty-five-year-old can usually recover from investment mistakes, but if you make those same mistakes as a sixty-five-year-old, when you're dependent on your investments for monthly income, it can be financially fatal.

Investor Behavior

Warren Buffet was quoted as saying, "It won't be the economy that will do in investors; it will be investors themselves." The absolute, hands-down, single most important determining factor in the success or failure of any investment plan is the behavior of the investor. No other determinant—or, for that matter, all other determinants combined—will impact a portfolio as much as investor behavior. Whether it's the disciplined, calculated approach embraced by the experienced professional or the spontaneous, irrational buying and selling evidenced by the amateur, investor behavior determines the underlying success or failure of any investment program.

I bring this point up now because all of the principles and strategies previously discussed in this chapter, even if implemented with

---

Brochure, 2009, 1.

perfection, are meaningless if you, as an investor, abandon the plan. Nick Murray succinctly describes the creation, implementation, and subsequent abandonment of an investment plan as "rearranging the deck chairs on the Titanic."[18] Unfortunately, I see a lot of Titanic deck-chair rearranging going on.

Every experienced investor knows that investment success isn't about making all of the right moves; it's really about making the least mistakes. Only a goal-focused investment plan will help maintain the discipline necessary to achieve your retirement income goals.[19]

---

18. Nick Murray, *Simple Wealth, Inevitable Wealth* (Southold, NY: Nick Murray Company, 1999), 145.

19. Investing involved risk, including loss of principal. An investor's shares, when redeemed may be worth less or more than the original investment price. An investor should carefully consider the investment objectives, risks, charges, and expenses of a mutual fund before investing. The fund prospectus contains this and other information about the fund. Contact your advisor or the fund company for a copy of the prospectus, which should be read carefully before investing.

CHAPTER 9

ANNUITIES

A discussion about retirement income planning can't take place without the words "annuity" or "annuitization" somehow being thrown into the conversation. Annuities are some of the most misunderstood planning tools available to the retiree today, but, if used properly, they can provide guarantees unavailable in any other product.

There are many different kinds of annuities; they come in all shapes, sizes, and flavors. All annuities, however, have two things in common: they (1) are issued and backed by insurance companies, and (2) are risk management tools that provide some type of guarantee to the purchaser usually in the form of a guaranteed stream of income, a guaranteed interest rate, or a guaranteed death benefit.

Essentially, when you purchase an annuity, the underlying insurance company that issues the annuity contract is taking on some of the risk previously borne by the purchaser of the annuity. Of course, this comes at a price.

It is important to note that the annuity guarantees discussed in this chapter are only as strong as the insurance companies that sell the annuities. Therefore, you must examine not only the features and costs of individual annuity contracts, but also the financial strength of the insurance companies providing them. Independent rating agencies such as A.M. Best, Moody, and Fitch can help in the process.

I find it interesting that annuities are such polarizing products. Some people in the financial profession demonize annuities and would never use them. Others consider annuities a cure-all product, using them exclusively as the solution to all investment needs. In my opinion, both extremes of the annuity debate are wrong. Annuities are niche players; they can be an effective part of a retirement income solution, but they should never be sold as the entire solution. A common-sense discussion of the features, guarantees, and costs of various types of annuities is necessary, because they may play an important part of some retirement income plans.

Annuity Types and Guarantees

There are several annuity types and guarantees, and it's important to understand their differences before using them.

The Immediate Annuity

The immediate annuity is purchased with a lump sum of money from the investor. The insurance company exchanges this lump-sum payment for a stream of guaranteed income to the investor. This stream of income may last for a specific number of payments, or it may last a lifetime depending on the terms of the specific annuity contract. The process of exchanging a lump sum of money for a stream of payments is called *annuitization*. Annuitization is the opposite of life insurance. When you buy life insurance, you cover the risk of dying too soon; when you purchase an immediate annuity for life, you're covering the risk of living too long. In chapter 1, I mentioned a 108-year-old client with whom I work. He purchased an immediate annuity years ago that guaranteed him an income for life. He has been systematically receiving monthly payments now for about thirty years, twenty years longer than the insurance company probably expected to pay him the immediate annuity payment when they promised him income for the rest of his life.

Essentially, defined benefit pension payments are immediate annuities. Social Security payments could likewise be classified as annuitized payments with survivor benefits. The academic world recognizes the importance of immediate annuities and the guaranteed stream of income they provide. They are becoming more important today, as the guaranteed pension payments of past generations are no longer available to most of today's retirees.

The Fixed Annuity

Fixed annuities are investments that accumulate a guaranteed interest rate for a specified period of time. Money within fixed annuities grows tax-deferred, unlike interest earned on a bank account or other taxable investments. Interest on fixed annuities is not taxable until it is actually withdrawn from the annuity. Fixed annuities are backed by insurance companies and limited state insurance guarantee funds, unlike bank deposits, which are guaranteed by the FDIC. Remember, the guarantee an insurance company offers is only as strong as the company itself. For that reason, the financial soundness of the underlying insurance company issuing the fixed annuity contract must be considered before purchase. Fixed annuities can be annuitized like immediate annuities, but in my experience, most investors do not exercise that option.

The Variable Annuity

Variable annuities are similar to fixed annuities in the sense that they grow tax-deferred, but that's where the similarities end. The underlying investments for variable annuities are not guaranteed by an insurance company; rather, they are tied to multiple investment options called *subaccounts*, which the purchaser chooses. Subaccounts are created by investment companies, and they can be managed either conservatively or aggressively, depending on the objective. Every variable annuity contract will offer investors anywhere from a dozen to as many as one hundred subaccount choices in which to allocate their investment dollars.

I liken a variable annuity to a buffet-style restaurant. You pay a fee to get into the buffet, then choose the entrées that most appeal to you. Likewise, once you own a variable annuity, you can transfer between subaccounts and change them without additional charges or taxation. The word "variable" refers both to the fact that you can pick and choose from a wide variety of subaccounts, and to the fact that the performance is variable depending on the underlying returns of the subaccounts you select.

Variable annuities have two primary guarantee features that can be added at additional costs: the *death benefit guarantee* and the *guaranteed minimum withdrawal benefit* (GMWB).

Death Benefit Guarantee

The death benefit guarantee offers a safety net to the beneficiaries of the deceased annuity owner. It allows variable annuity beneficiaries to transfer investment risk to the issuing insurance company. This is done by guaranteeing the original principal, or by guaranteeing the original principal plus an annual interest rate increase on monies invested at the death of the annuity owner. Of course, if the account balance at death is higher than the guarantee, the beneficiary will receive the account balance. For example, let's say Richard invests $100,000 into a variable annuity with a 5-percent-increase-per-year death benefit guarantee and dies after five years. Let's further assume that Richard invests in a high-risk subaccount within the variable annuity and that he loses 30 percent of his investment value during those five years. Upon his death, even though his $100,000 has turned into $70,000 because of the 30 percent investment loss, Richard's beneficiaries will receive $125,000 because of the 5 percent death benefit guarantee that he had on his annuity. How?

$$\$100,000 \times 5\% \times 5 \text{ years} = \$125,000$$

The Death Benefit Guarantee:
John and Jackie

John worked for a state university and had accumulated $234,700 in his 401(k) before he was forced to retire because of Parkinson's disease. John had a pension with the state, Social Security income, and a good long-term care policy. Jackie worked so that they wouldn't need money out of John's retirement accumulation for the foreseeable future.

The Parkinson's disease was progressing rapidly, and John and Jackie decided to roll over the state retirement plan into a variable annuity with a 6 percent annual growth guarantee upon death. This assured that, upon John's death, his family would receive either the account balance or 6 percent per year growth on the principal invested, whichever was greater. In 2004, John invested the $234,700 into a 100 percent stock sub account, and why not? If the stock market were to take off, John and his family would reap the benefits. If the stock market went down, upon his death his family would have the 6 percent guaranteed growth of the principal.

John happened to die in March of 2009 at the bottom of the market crash of 2008–2009. His account value at the date of his death was $134,237 because of market losses. The insurance company paid Jackie $274,994 because of the death benefit guarantee that accompanied the variable annuity. That payment was over $40,000 more than the original investment and over $140,000 more than the annuity balance at the date of death.

Guaranteed Minimum Withdrawal Benefits (GMWBs)

The insurance industry understands the tremendous opportunity at their doorstep. Eighty million baby boomers are retiring and looking for investments that can provide both good rates of return and some kind of guarantee of income should the stock market fall on hard times. Under these circumstances, the *Guaranteed Minimum Withdrawal Benefits* were born.

GMWBs guarantee a minimum withdrawal amount from the variable annuity regardless of the annuity account balance. At a minimum, 100 percent of the money paid into the variable annuity will be returned to the purchaser over time. This allows the investor to invest aggressively inside the variable annuity, knowing that if markets go down, they'll recoup at least what they have paid into the annuity over a period of years. If markets go up, then the guarantees will not be necessary, and the variable annuity can be managed or liquidated as a lump sum, just like any other stock-based investment.

There are three components of GMWBs that need to be understood:

1. The protected or guaranteed balance
2. The withdrawal rate
3. The contract value or account value

The Protected Balance

The protected balance is the guaranteed amount of money the variable annuity owner can draw on during his or her lifetime. Initially, the protected balance is the amount of money invested in the variable annuity. Thereafter, every insurance company has its own provisions for increasing the protected balance. For example, if the actual account value of the variable annuity goes up in a given year, the protected balance can lock in those gains, creating a new, higher, protected balance known as a *step-up*. Some insurance companies will even step-up the protected balance by 6 percent or by the actual value of the variable annuity on its anniversary, whichever is greater.

The Withdrawal Rate

The insurance company is not going to allow the variable annuity owner to take the protected balance out in a lump sum. The withdrawal rate is the maximum amount per year that can be withdrawn from the protected balance while maintaining the GMWB guarantee. Typical withdrawal rates vary depending on the product and the age of the annuity owner, but they range from 4 percent to 7 percent annually. It is important to have a large protected balance, but equally important to have access to that protected balance through reasonable withdrawal rates.

The Contract Value or Account Value

The contract value is the actual current value of the subaccounts in the variable annuity. *It is important to note that the death benefit of the annuity or the contract value, whichever is greater, is what gets paid to the beneficiary, not the protected balance.* The protected balance is only used to gauge how much can be withdrawn during the annuity owner's life.

For a practical example, let's say Susan wants to invest in a portfolio of stocks but is concerned about potential market losses and the volatility of owning a 100-percent-stock mutual fund. She invests $100,000 into a 100-percent-stock subaccount with a GMWB and enjoys three years of good growth, seeing her variable annuity grow to $140,000. In the fourth year, however, the markets tank, and her account balance drops to $90,000. Because Susan's GMWB has an annual step-up, she is guaranteed to receive the highest contract anniversary value of $140,000 (her protected balance). Her contract states that she can only get 7 percent of the protected balance each year. If she abides by the 7 percent withdrawal rate, Susan will receive annual payments of $9,800 until all of the $140,000 is paid ($140,000 x 7% = $9,800 annually). If she had not purchased the GMWB, she would simply have had to live with the $90,000 account value.

GMWB: Alex and Norma

Alex and Norma loved volunteering as missionaries for their Christian church, and their missionary activities had taken them to India, China, and several other locations around the world.

While they were out of the country, their ability to actively communicate with me about their investments was often limited. Therefore, at my suggestion, they placed the stock portion of their IRA into a variable annuity with a Guaranteed Minimum Withdrawal Benefit (GMWB). They chose an annuity that allowed a 7 percent withdrawal amount per year. Additionally, the GMWB promised to step up the protected balance on every fifth anniversary if the account value were greater than the original protected balance. This benefit guaranteed that, even if their stock portfolio inside the variable annuity dropped to zero, they would get their original investment back over time, plus step-ups.

At the time they opted for the GMWB, their investment was $480,000. Their account balance grew to $764,000 in 2008, but during the recession of 2008–9, the contract value of their investment sank to $395,000. Had they not elected to use a GMWB, they would have simply lost $85,000 ($480,000-$395,000). But because they elected to use a GMWB, Alex and Norma will receive a total of $764,000 (the stepped-up fifth anniversary value) paid to them at the rate of $54,000 (7 percent) per year for fourteen years.

It is important to remember that the restrictions on how money is withdrawn from GMWB annuities are only imposed if the annuity has lost money and guarantees are needed.

Who Should Use GMWBs

GMWBs are complicated and vary greatly. This complexity is not intended to confuse you; rather, it's the natural evolution of a product created by actuaries who are charged to create a product that simultaneously appeals to the purchaser and protects the insurance company.

I find that analogies often help to explain difficult concepts, so I'll give it a try regarding GMWBs. Lake Powell is located in southern Utah, in one of the most hostile deserts in the United States. Temperatures typically reach over one hundred degrees daily from May through September. The lake was created by the Glen Canyon dam, which backs up the Colorado River through miles of red rock cliffs and canyons, making Lake Powell a recreational paradise enjoyed by a million visitors annually.

Even though the weather is hot, a cool, refreshing dive in the lake is always available. Occasionally, the area experiences violent thunderstorms, complete with torrential downpours, lightning, and microburst winds, which can make Lake Powell a dangerous place for inexperienced boaters and swimmers. Wearing a life jacket while swimming in the lake is not mandatory. Some swimmers who are confident in their skills don't wear life jackets, because they feel they don't need them; they get in the way, and besides, a good life jacket can be expensive.

On the other extreme are those people who don't want to get in the water at all. These are swimmers who feel they lack the swimming experience and ability to survive in a large, deep lake like Lake Powell. Most of these people will get in the lake only if they have a life jacket—otherwise, forget it. They would rather bake in the 110-degree heat than risk drowning. In doing so, they open themselves up to all sorts of other hazards like dehydration, sunburns, and heatstroke.

The swimmers who are in the most danger in the lake are those who don't think they need a life jacket, but who lack the necessary experience when thunderstorms, winds, and waves appear. These self-confident yet unprepared individuals occasionally drown because of a lack of preparation, a lack of true experience, and the inability to make good decisions in stressful situations.

GMWBs are like the life jackets in the analogy. The water is the stock markets, and the thunderstorms are volatile market conditions. The swimmers are obviously the investors. Just as truly experienced swimmers probably don't need life jackets, experienced investors don't need the guarantees of GMWBs; after all, they really can get in the way and add an unnecessary expense. Experienced investors have made it through numerous market corrections before, and they're prepared to manage the occasional annoying volatile market. Besides, financial thunderstorms usually last a short while.

For the inexperienced, the GMWB life jacket is essential. Without the life jacket, the inexperienced would stay out of the water (the stock market) altogether, which, in the nonstop heat of the desert (inflation), would eventually cause death—they might not drown, but they'd certainly wither away. Only the life jacket provides them with the confidence they need to get into the lifesaving water.

The investor who feels comfortable with stocks but panics at the occasional and unpredictable stormy market is also a person who should consider a GMWB guarantee. If the GMWB keeps this investor from making financially fatal decisions in a moment of irrational fear, then the extra costs of a variable annuity with a GMWB are well justified.

If you're a risk-averse investor, you may want to consider purchasing a variable annuity with a GMWB rider. As previously discussed, it is virtually impossible to keep up with inflation by relying solely on safe investments such as bonds and CDs. Stocks must be a part of a retirement strategy, even if they only play a small part. The problem, as I see it, is that there are many retirees who simply can't stand the volatility of the stock market and who therefore avoid stocks altogether—or worse, limp out of them when the markets lose 30 percent, as markets have done historically about every fifth year.[1]

If a variable annuity with a GMWB could convince a retiree to take on more risk and invest in stocks when he otherwise might have stayed invested in a CD, then in the long term, the extra expenses associated with the variable annuity with a GMWB are justified. If it keeps the investor from making monumental mistakes such as panicking and withdrawing from stocks at the bottom of a market decline, then the extra expense of the GMWB is likewise justified.

If you aren't a risk-averse investor—if you believe the market's downturns are cyclical and have the patience, experience, and time to ride out the sometimes extreme volatility in the stock markets—you probably shouldn't invest in a variable annuity with a GMWB. Historically, if investors are patient during down markets, they are rewarded. After all, markets have always rebounded; sometimes it takes several years, but the markets have never stayed down permanently.

GMWB Recommendations

There are five recommendations that I'd suggest to anyone considering a variable annuity with a GMWB benefit.

1. Only invest the most aggressive part of an investment portfolio into an annuity with a GMWB. Even though safer subaccounts are available in variable annuities with GMWBs, don't use them. The expenses within a variable annuity with a GMWB are too high to invest into relatively safe subaccounts, such as bonds. Safe money should be invested elsewhere in accounts with lower fees.

---

1. Historically, there is a market correction every fifth year on the average, but past performance is no guarantee of future results.

2. Understand and abide by the withdrawal restrictions associated with a GMWB. Otherwise, you may pay a lot for a GMWB benefit but gain little. For example, if the withdrawal limit is 7 percent annually, and you withdraw 10 percent, the guarantees associated with the GMWB (the protected balance) can disappear, but the extra annual cost associated with that benefit remains. Read and understand the fine print.

3. Only purchase GMWBs from top-rated insurance companies. The guarantees are only as strong as the insurance company issuing the variable annuity contract.

4. Carefully analyze the benefits and associated costs of each GMWB guarantee. Prior to the market crash of 2008–9, GMWB benefits were less costly and more generous in their guarantees than the GMWBs of today. Since the market correction, the insurance industry has universally reduced guarantees and increased the costs of these benefits, to the point that I wonder whether the GMWB guarantees available in many variable annuities today are worth the extra costs associated with them. If this trend continues in the future, the cost of these guarantees will outweigh their benefits.

5. Not all GMWB guarantees are created equal. It is important to compare guarantees and cost of GMWBs between companies before purchasing a GMWB rider. In other words, shop around.

Disadvantages of Variable Annuities

The disadvantages of variable annuities are the costs, the lack of liquidity, and the fact that they are sometimes used in situations where they do not belong.

Costs

Variable annuities come with insurance, or guarantees against losses, and where there is insurance, there is always an insurance premium. Costs associated with optional riders, such as a GMWB or death benefit rider, are in addition to the base cost of a variable annuity and typically range anywhere from 0.3 to 1.35 percent, depending on the benefit. These costs are added onto the variable annuity base cost of a 1 to 1.7 percent annual fee. Therefore, the total cost of a variable annuity with a GMWB rider can easily exceed 3 percent. That's double the average costs associated with comparable types of investments.

Those Fees Add Up

When comparing investments, fees must be taken into consideration. You wouldn't think that a fee of 1.5 percent versus 3 percent would make much of a difference. Well, it does.

Let's compare two investments. "Investment A" gets an 8 percent rate of return on $500,000 with a modest 1.5 percent fee. "Investment B" gets the same 8 percent return as "Investment A," except it carries a 3 percent fee.

	Growth of Investment A 8% gross return -1.5% fee =6.5% net	Growth of Investment B 8% gross return -3% fee =5% net	Net Difference In Value
10 years	$ 938,569	$ 814, 447	$ 124,122
20 years	$ 1,769, 822	$ 1,326, 649	$ 435, 173
30 years	$ 3,307,183	$ 2,106,971	$ 1, 146, 212

fig. 9.1

It's shocking to see that the 1.5 percent extra cost associated with the GMWB and death benefit guarantees would result in a greater than $1 million difference between Investment A and B over a thirty-year retirement (see fig. 9.1). You have to ask yourself: Do I really need all those guarantees? As you can see, they cost a lot of money, so use them sparingly.

I believe it's valid to argue that the expenses of variable annuities with GMWBs and death benefit guarantees can be justified if the extra protection allows the owner to invest more aggressively, thereby generating higher returns over the long run to offset the extra costs. Research has shown that purchasers of variable annuities with a GMWB do indeed invest more aggressively than investors without guarantees.

Lack of Liquidity

Some variable annuities are not as accessible as other types of investments. Variable annuities sold by commission-based investment professionals (registered representatives) usually impose back-end surrender charges if liquidated within a certain time period. These surrender periods typically last four to seven years, and the charges can be as high as 8.5 percent of the value of the variable annuity upon liquidation.

If a variable annuity is desired, a better alternative would be to acquire the annuity through a fee-based advisor (an RIA). Variable annuities complete with GMWBs and death-benefit guarantees purchased through RIAs are 100 percent liquid and impose no fee upon withdrawal.

All variable annuities, whether purchased through registered representatives or RIAs, have annual fees associated with them. The surrender charges can be avoided, however, by investing into a variable annuity through an RIA.[2]

---

2. See chapter twelve for a more complete explanation of the different types of financial professionals.

Sold Where Not Suitable

Variable annuities are sold by insurance companies, and many times, they are the only investment products that the insurance agents who work for those companies sell. I often come across clients who own variable annuity investments when a cheaper, more liquid alternative would have done a better job. Buyer beware! If the only solution your financial representative shows you is a variable annuity, that's probably a good sign that it's time to find a different financial representative.

Before purchasing a variable annuity, ask yourself, "Why do I want or need a variable annuity? And how much will it cost me?" If the answer is to defer taxes or to obtain a guaranteed death benefit or a guaranteed minimum withdrawal benefit, a variable annuity is probably an intelligent purchase as long as you understand and accept the costs. If these aren't the reasons for your purchase, then you can probably find a different investment product that will provide you more investment options, fewer charges, and more liquidity than a variable annuity.

A Concluding Note

I recognize that variable annuities with guarantees cost more than alternatives such as mutual funds, and I'm not suggesting that the costs associated with variable annuities with GMWBs and death benefits are cheap—they're not. Variable annuities with guarantees cost extra because they transfer your risk to an insurance company.

I have worked with retirees for almost a quarter of a century, and I know of very few individuals who, at age seventy-five (with a possible life expectancy of twenty-plus more years) can stand the wild swings associated with the stock market in even a small portion of their portfolio without some sort of guarantee. In my estimates, the costs of the GMWB and death benefit guarantee are unbelievably less expensive than avoiding stocks altogether and running out of money during retirement due to inflation. GMWBs are also immeasurably less expensive than selling out of stocks in a panic when the market declines 40 percent and hiding the diminished balance in a bank account systematically losing value due to inflation. If purchased prudently by risk-averse retirees, the variable annuity with a death benefit and/or GMWB can play an important part of a retirement income plan.

Investors should carefully consider a variable annuity's risks, charges, limitations, and expenses, as well as the risks, charges, expenses, and investment objectives of the underlying investment options. This and other information is provided in the product and underlying fund prospectuses. Please contact the annuity company or your advisor to obtain a copy of these prospectuses. Read them carefully before investing.

Annuities are long-term investments designed for retirement purposes. Product features and availability may vary by state. Withdrawals of taxable amounts are subject to income tax, and if taken prior to age fifty-nine and one-half, a 10 percent federal tax penalty may apply. Early withdrawals may be subject to withdrawal changes. Optional riders are available at an additional cost. All guarantees are based on the claims-paying ability of the insurer. An annuity is a tax-deferred investment. Holding an annuity, IRA, or other qualified account offers no additional tax benefit. Therefore, an annuity should be used to fund an IRA or qualified plan for annuity features other than tax deferral.

An insurer's financial strength rating represents an opinion by the issuing agency regarding the ability of an insurance company to meet its financial obligations to its policyholders and contract holders. A rating is an opinion of the rating agency only, and not a statement of fact or recommendation to purchase, sell, or hold any security, policy, or contract. There ratings do not imply approval of a product and do not reflect any indication of its performance. For more information about a particular rating or rating agency, please visit the website of the relevant agency.

CHAPTER 10

WITHDRAWAL STRATEGIES

Some retirees may have enough income from Social Security and pensions to avoid systematic withdrawals from their personal investments. Others may only need to dip into this source of income for special expenses, such as a vacation or the occasional new car. I find most retirees, however, require a steady flow of income from their investment portfolio to sustain them during retirement.

One of the most difficult parts of the retirement income planning process is coming up with a sustainable withdrawal strategy from your investments and sticking with it. Developing a withdrawal strategy can be complicated, but it is one of the most important aspects of retirement income planning; perhaps even as important as how the investment portfolio is actually invested. A retirement income withdrawal strategy has two main components:

- **The Withdrawal Rate:** How much to take out of investments annually.

- **Withdrawal Methodology:** How to structure investments to provide the growth and income necessary to last
through retirement, and how to turn these investments
into monthly income.

The good news is that a competent retirement income planner can
combine academic research regarding income-producing strategies
with appropriate investment products to produce the inflation-
adjusted flow of income necessary for the retiree.

Withdrawal Rates

Prior to the huge market downturns of 2000–2 and, more
recently, the downturns of 2008–9, many retirees were misled
into making overly optimistic withdrawals during their early
retirement years. Their experiences with high-returning investment portfolios from 1982 to 2000 led retirees to believe that
annual withdrawal rates of 7 percent to 8 percent would leave
their portfolios' values virtually unchanged or even allow for
growth The severity of corrections experienced during the first
decade of the twenty-first century has exposed this fallacy. Many
of the retirees who awarded themselves these generous withdrawal rates now find themselves having to cut back on their
lifestyles dramatically; some are even being forced to go back to
work to supplement their retirement income.

However, during this decade, many academic researchers have
addressed the following question: How much income can and
should be appropriately withdrawn from retirement funds? I wish
the answer were simple, but it isn't. A sustainable withdrawal rate
is a function of two factors. The time horizon over which income
is needed and the underlying investment mix both affect what
withdrawal rate may be appropriate; therefore, changes in the time
horizon or investment allocation affect how much you can safely
withdraw from investments over a retirement period.

PROBABILITY OF MEETING INCOME NEEDS OVER 25 YEARS

ASSET ALLOCATIONS	INITIAL WITHDRAWL RATE			
	3%	4%	5%	6%
	PROBABILITY OF SUCCESS			
US STOCKS - 100%	99%	92%	81%	68%
US STOCKS - 75% US BONDS - 25%	98%	94%	83%	66%
US STOCKS - 50% US BONDS - 50%	99%	97%	83%	57%
US STOCKS - 25% US BONDS - 75%	99%	97%	73%	30%
US BONDS - 100%	94%	85%	33%	4%

fig. 10.1 For illustrative purposes only. Not a recommendation of any specific asset allocation strategy.
Sources: Data from Transamerica, 2008; Morningstar, *Probability of Meeting Income Needs*, 2008; Franklin Templeton Investments, 2008.

Almost all academic research concurs that no more than a 5 percent withdrawal rate is appropriate based upon a moderately allocated portfolio. Again, I must emphasize that you need to include at least limited to moderate exposure to stocks in your portfolio, to increase your probability of a successful distribution strategy. As illustrated in fig. 10.1, an ultraconservative portfolio will not keep up with inflation and will cripple your chances of success.

Once you decide on a withdrawal percentage, it is imperative to have the discipline to stick to that percentage. New retirees usually have far larger account balances at their disposal than they've ever had before. Many times, I have seen the urge to buy a new fifth-wheel trailer or a second home, or even the urge to help a financially struggling child, take precedence over a disciplined withdrawal percentage. Their rationale is: *Why not spend some of my hard-earned dollars now? After all, I've been saving for my retirement, and now I'm retired.* The problem, of course, is that without a disciplined strategy, some retirees blow through investable assets in the first ten years of a thirty-year retirement and spend the last two decades of retirement cash-strapped and solely dependent on their Social Security checks.

Withdrawal Methodology

One of the most common and disastrous mistakes in planning retirement income is to base withdrawal plans on historical averages and project those averages in a linear manner for a thirty-year retirement. So, before jumping into withdrawal strategies, you must understand why using averages to calculate retirement income streams is deeply flawed and dangerous. The problem with averages is that they are derived from a series of numbers, both higher and lower, that do not resemble the "average" very much. For example, according to Ibbotson it is true that the S&P 500, or large U.S. stocks, have averaged a 9.9 percent return from 1926 to 2010.[1] But rarely did the *annual* return come close to the 9.9 percent average for that time period. The majority of the years posted either negative returns or returns in excess of 20 percent. On an annual basis, the large stocks that produced a 9.9 percent average return have fluctuated from a high of 54 percent to a low of -43 percent.

Projecting returns in a linear manner based on averages is like deciding to wade across a river that is, on average, four feet deep. The average may be four feet, but that won't help you when you're in the middle of a section ten feet deep. Planning retirement income streams based on linear projections of average returns can very easily create a misleading sense of security about a portfolio's chance of success.

---

1. Ibbotson and Sinquefield, *SBBI 2010 Yearbook.*

The challenge of creating a successful withdrawal program is threefold:

1. How do you successfully create income from non-income-producing assets, such as stocks in 401(k)s and IRAs?

2. How do you create an income plan that effectively keeps up with inflation?

3. How do you avoid as much market risk as possible and keep from self-destructing due to fear or greed during volatile market swings?

Let's examine the strengths and weaknesses of common withdrawal strategies.

The Interest-Only Strategy

This strategy involves investing a lump sum of money into fixed-income-producing assets such as bonds, money market accounts, fixed annuities, and CDs, and then living solely off of the interest. The advantages to this strategy are clear:

1. Little or no market risk

2. Steady income

3. Simple to implement and manage

Unfortunately, these advantages are far outweighed by the disadvantages. First, very few individuals have enough money to make this a viable income option. In today's low-interest-rate environment, it would take millions of dollars to produce a reasonable income. One million dollars invested in a portfolio of bonds yielding 4 percent would produce only $40,000 of annual income. Second, even if an individual has substantial wealth to dedicate to this income strategy, the strategy itself does not keep up with inflation. Unless the retiree is planning on a short life span, the strategy won't work. Again, any strategy that avoids stocks altogether will not keep up with inflation.

The "Annuitize Everything" Strategy

Remember, when a person annuitizes, he or she trades a lump sum of money for a stream of guaranteed payments. Some retirees choose to annuitize pension payments (instead of rolling the pension to an IRA) because they simply don't want to worry about managing the money, or because they want to guarantee a monthly pension payment during retirement.

Initially the idea of guaranteed income without market risk sounds pretty good, but again, inflation keeps this from being a viable option. Remember, at a 3 percent inflation rate, one dollar will have the purchasing power of thirty cents thirty years from now. Therefore, that $4,000 guaranteed monthly payment today will have the equivalent purchasing power of only $1,200 in thirty years. Additionally, you can't access that annuitized lump sum of money in case of emergencies, and you can't pass it on to your heirs.

I'm not saying retirement money should never be annuitized. In fact, in certain circumstances, it makes sense that part of a retirement income plan would consist of this type of guaranteed monthly income. But remember that growth, in addition to income, is a vital component of a retirement income plan. Annuitization by itself, without a growth component such as stocks, is destined to fail because of inflation.

Systematic Withdrawal from a Balanced Portfolio

This method of withdrawal is by far the most popular. It entails investing retirement funds across a diversified mix of investments: stocks, bonds, real estate, and so on, taking systematic withdrawals and then rebalancing that portfolio on a regular basis. This method of investing is entirely appropriate for the accumulation of retirement funds, but it has some potential pitfalls during the distribution phase. When you're an accumulator, down markets are actually opportunities to purchase beaten-up investments at bargain prices; you can always simply wait for markets to rebound. But when you're a distributor, selling depleted assets to provide monthly income during declining markets can be devastating.

If bear markets prevail in the early years of a lengthy retirement, the retiree will never recover money lost, even in the most diversified portfolio. The inverse is also true: if bull markets prevail during the first part of a lengthy retirement, account balances will grow and there will likely be more-than-sufficient income to fund a retirement. The problem is no one can determine the timing of bull markets and bear markets. Essentially, systematic withdrawals from a balanced portfolio are a game of chance; a roll of the dice that most retirees would reject if they understood the odds.

If the retiree chooses systematic withdrawals from a balanced portfolio, the question is, will the retiree be lucky enough to retire on the right day? Let's assume Mr. Red and Mr. Green both retired with $500,000 and invest their retirement funds in a 60 percent stock and 40 percent bond allocation. Furthermore, they each withdrew $25,000, or 5% annually and increased the withdrawal amount by the annual inflation rate. The only discrepancy in their strategies is the date they decided to retire. Mr. Red retired on January 1, 1966, and Mr. Green retired on January 1, 1976 (see figure 10.2).

ARE YOU LUCKY ENOUGH TO RETIRE
ON THE RIGHT DAY?

Mr. Green
$500.000
Stock 60% Bonds 40%
Annual Withdrawals: $25,000
Retired 1/1/1976

Mr. Red
$500.000
Stock 60% Bonds 40%
Annual Withdrawals: $25,000
Retired 1/1/1966

		Mr. Green		
Age	Year	RoR *	Year-end Value
65	1976	20.9%	$518,059
66	1977	-5.5%	$518,106
67	1978	2.1%	$498,689
68	1979	9.4%	$511,830
69	1980	15.2	$551,338
70	1981	-1.5%	$500,828
71	1982	29.3	$602,729
72	1983	13.5%	$637,815
73	1984	9.5%	$650,127
74	1985	30.7%	$799,715
75	1986	24.1%	$941,517
76	1987	0.4%	$892,495
77	1988	13.5%	$958,010
78	1989	27.8%	$1,166,716
79	1990	0.3%	$1,109,482
80	1991	25.1%	$1,324,672
81	1992	8.9%	$1,377,373
82	1993	14.0%	$1,503,058
83	1994	-3.7%	$1,378,579
84	1995	35.3%	$1,794,399
85	1996	14.0%	$1,972,706
86	1997	25.6%	$2,403,137
87	1998	23.5%	$2,892,131
88	1999	8.9%	$3,072,114

		Mr. Red		
Age	Year	RoR *	Year-end Value
65	1966	- 5.3%	$447,786
66	1967	12.8%	$478,594
67	1968	7.3%	$485,913
68	1969	-8.0%	$417,913
69	1970	9.4%	$426,403
70	1971	12.7%	$448,413
71	1972	13.6%	$476,223
72	1973	-9.8%	$394,315
73	1974	-15.2%	$295,252
74	1975	23.3%	$321,347
75	1976	20.9%	$343,350
76	1977	-5.5%	$276,371
77	1978	2.1%	$230,428
78	1979	9.4%	$194,470
79	1980	15.2%	$158,632
80	1981	-1.5%	$84,110
81	1982	29.3%	$32,167
82	1983	13.5%	Exhausted

Unfortunately, Mr. Red
ran out of money in less
than 17 years.

*RoR = Rate of Return

fig. 10.2 Each portfolio assumes a first-year, 5 percent withdrawal that was subsequently adjusted for actual inflation and then rebalanced annually. Stocks are represented by the S&P 500. Bonds are represented by the annualized yields of long-term Treasuries (which have a ten-year maturity). Inflation is represented by changes to historical CPI. This illustration does not account for any taxes or fees. Source: Data from John Hancock, 2009.[2]

2. Illustrative purposes only; the hypothetical returns do not reflect an actual investment.

Mr. Green was fortunate enough to retire at the front end of a bull market, which provided him with more money than he will probably ever need. Mr. Red, on the other hand, had unfortunate timing. He retired at the beginning of a bear market and ran out of money in seventeen years.

You will find that many investment professionals use this withdrawal strategy, as shortsighted as it is. You may be thinking, "There has got to be a better way." Well, there is. It is called time segmentation.

The Time-Segmented Distribution Strategy

A visitor to a Christmas tree farm will quickly notice that the growth of the trees is staggered. Some of the trees are ready to harvest now, while the rest of the trees are given time to grow to maturity. Some will be ready to harvest next year, some in five years, and some in ten years. The point is that the tree farm has implemented a plan so that they'll always be able to produce mature trees for future income.

Time-segmented investing works like a Christmas tree farm. At Peterson Financial, we segment retirement funds into six five-year periods. For example, segment number one will provide monthly income for years one through five; segment two will provide income for years six through ten; segment three for years eleven through fifteen, and so on, until thirty years of retirement income are covered. Separating assets in this way allows us to pursue different goals with each segment and diversify risk in a way that is designed to help protect our client's short-term income while giving the stock markets time to work over the long term.

Money invested in segment one will provide income for the first five years of retirement. Safety is the most important objective of this segment. There simply cannot be any market risk associated with segment one, because guaranteed monthly income is the goal. Typically, money in segment one is invested in a CD or an immediate annuity—again, something with guarantees. Segment six, on the other hand, is designed to provide income for years twenty-five through thirty of retirement and should be invested for growth in a diversified stock portfolio. Segments four, five, and six are all inflation fighters. These segments will have volatility, but they won't be needed for income for fifteen to twenty-five years. Of course, you might worry that the stock markets will crash and then stay down for fifteen to twenty-five years. But history has shown that the risk of investing in stocks decreases over the length of time that the stocks are held. So is holding stocks for fifteen to twenty years adequate to stave off major risks?

To answer this question, remember that stocks are volatile in the short run. That's why you don't buy stocks if you have a short time horizon, such as five years. Again, since 1926 the range for stock returns for a one-year holding period ranges from a high of 54 percent to a low of -43 percent. The average range for a five-year holding period encompasses a high of 29 percent and a low of -12 percent. Remarkably, however, for a twenty-year holding period, the range is between an 18 percent high and a 3 percent low. There has never been a twenty-year holding period where a diversified portfolio of large stocks has lost money. This fact is a reminder that stock ownership is an essential ingredient in your retirement income plan if you want to have an inflation-adjusted flow of income to last throughout retirement. At the same time, it is reassuring to know that the money you've invested in stocks won't be needed for a long time, and that, historically, holding stocks over a long period of time has proved favorable.

Given that an inflation-adjusted stream of income for thirty years is the ultimate goal of a retirement income plan, each segment should be individually monitored and harvested to safeguard future income. The term "harvested" means that the retiree sells out of more risky investments and moves to safer investments once the goals of each segment have been realized.

For example, Tom divides his retirement funds into six segments and, during the eighth year of his retirement, while enjoying regular income from segment two (which provides income for years six through ten), the market surges. Segments three and four reach their growth goals and will be able to provide the planned income for their respective time segments. Therefore, Tom "harvests" these stocks by liquidating them and moving them to more conservative investments.

Computer programs aid the financial advisor in (1) determining how much retirement money should be invested in each segment, and (2) monitoring each segment's progress toward its growth goal.

Some may say that by harvesting, we may be taking money out of the market prematurely, preventing any potential future gains beyond the goal. However, our goal is not to maximize growth, but rather to provide inflation-adjusted income at the lowest possible risk. The time-segmenting approach is goal-oriented, and it's the least risky way I know of to provide a stream of income throughout thirty years of retirement. I know of no available single strategy that can produce the predictability that this approach provides. For more information on time-segmented distribution, please watch the *Income for Life*® movie on my Web site, at http://www.speterson.retirementtime.com.[3]

---

3. The two main risks related to bond investing are interest rate risk and credit risk. Typically, when interest rates rise, there is a corresponding decline in the market value of bonds. Credit risk refers to the possibility that the issuer of the bond will not be able make principal and interest payments.

CDs are FDIC insured up to $250,000, and offer a fixed rate of return. They do not necessarily protect against a rising cost of living. The FDIC insurance on CDs applies in the case of bank insolvency, but does not protect market value.

Investing involves risk, including loss of principal. An investor's shares, when redeemed, may be worth less or more than the original investment price. An investor should carefully consider the investment objectives, risks, charges, and expenses of a mutual fund before investing. The fund prospectus contains this and other information about the fund. Contact your advisor or the fund company for a copy of the prospectus, which should be read carefully before investing.

An investment in a money market fund is not FDIC insured or guaranteed by any other government agency. Although the fund seeks to preserve the value of your investment at $1.00 per share, it is possible to lose money by investing in the fund.

Immediate fixed annuities are long-term investments designed for retirement purposes. Generally, a portion of each annuity payment is a tax-free return of your investment in the contract, and the remaining portion is taxable as ordinary income. Once your investment in the contract has been fully recovered, the remaining portion is subject to tax as ordinary income. If you are under age fifty-nine and one-half, a 10 percent tax penalty may also apply. All guarantees are based on the claims-paying ability of the insurer.

Stock and bond values fluctuate in price so that the value of an investment can go down depending on market conditions. Stock prices may fluctuate due to stock market volatility and market cycles, as well as circumstances specific to the company. The two main risks related to fixed income investing are interest rate risk and credit risk. Typically, when interest rates rise, there is corresponding decline in the market value of bonds. Credit risk refers to the possibility that the issuer of the bond will not be able to make principal and interest payments. Investments in higher-yielding, lower-rated corporate bonds are subject to greater fluctuations in value and risk of loss of income and principal.

The FDIC protects depositors against the loss of their deposits if an FDIC-insured bank or savings association fails. FDIC deposit insurance covers the balance of each depositor's account, dollar-for-dollar, up to the insurance limit, including principal and any accrued interest, through the date of the insured bank's closing. The standard insurance amount of $250,000 per depositor is in effect through December 31, 2013. On January 1, 2014, the standard insurance amount will return to $100,000 per depositor for all account categories except IRAs and other certain retirement accounts, which will remain at $250,000 per depositor. The FDIC coverage does not include securities or mutual funds.

CHAPTER 11

PUTTING IT ALL
TOGETHER

This book has focused on the financial challenges and opportunities that lie ahead for today's retiring baby boomers. The challenges of inflation, longevity, and investment management risk are ever present. At the same time, there are multiple opportunities and methods with which to squeeze the most out of each of the sources of retirement income, namely, Social Security, pensions, employment, reverse mortgages, and investment income.

Again, the objective of a retirement income plan is to provide an inflation-adjusted return to last throughout a long retirement (at least thirty years). The plan should be goal-oriented, easy to monitor and adjust, and designed to provide the maximum amount of income with the least amount of risk. The plan should be pragmatic and systematic in order to limit the damaging effects of individual behavior, namely fear and greed.

Let's look at three different couples in various situations who retired during the last couple of years to show how they, along with their retirement income planner, structured their retirement income plans.

Situation One: Ben and Darla

Ben, sixty-seven, and Darla, sixty-three, are both in good health and are looking forward to a long retirement together, exploring the backcountry in their four-wheel-drive Jeep. Ben worked for a gas company for thirty-two years, and Darla worked as a stay-at-home mom. Their home is paid for, and they figure they need $6,000 per month of inflation-adjusted income to maintain their lifestyle. Fig. 10.3 illustrates their sources of income.

Sources of Income	Total Monthly Income
Income Goal: $6,000	
Source of Income 1: Social Security	
Ben's Social Security benefit will be $2,305 per month, because he has waited to apply until after his full retirement age. Ben could get more Social Security if he waited until age seventy, but he wants to start his Social Security income now. Darla never worked outside of the home, but she's entitled to a portion of Ben's benefit as his spouse. She will receive $845, less than the 50 percent of Ben's benefit of $2,305 because she's applying for her spousal benefit at age sixty-three, three years short of her full retirement age. If she had waited until age sixty-six, she would have received $1,153 monthly, $308 more than she now receives. $2,305 + $845= $3,150	$3,150

Source of Income 2: Pension Plan	
The gas company offers Ben a pension plan, which rewards him for his thirty-two years of service. Because Ben wants Darla to be taken care of after his death, he considers the 100 percent joint and survivor option his only acceptable pension option. This would provide $2,899 monthly throughout both of their lives. Ben also considers buying an insurance policy to maximize his pension, but after running the numbers, he realizes it won't work out very well in his situation. After considering all his pension options, Ben decides to take the lump sum of $420,000 and roll it into an IRA, where it can be managed for future use. We can estimate the income from the lump sum by multiplying the lump sum by .05, or 5 percent $420,000 x .05 = $21,000 / 12 months = $1,750$ Remember, 5 percent is the maximum safe withdrawal percentage that should be used. Furthermore, upon their deaths, any residual money would pass to their heirs.	$1,750

Source of Income 3: Employment During Retirement	
Ben does not need to work during retirement, but he will have plenty of opportunity to work as a consultant to the gas company if he so decides. Ben does not want to figure employment income into their retirement income plan.	$0

Source of Income 4: Reverse Mortgage	
Ben and Darla worked hard to pay off their house and do not want to consider using any of the equity in their home for living expenses. However, they recognize this as an additional source of retirement income should they, for some reason, need extra money.	$0

Source of Income 5: Investment Income	
Ben has contributed to a 401(k) since he started working at the gas company. He has accumulated $348,000, and, given the 5 percent rule, he should be able to receive $1,450 of monthly income from the 401(k) values. $348,000 x .05 = $17,400 $17,400 / 12 months = $1,450 per month	$1,450
Total Monthly Income	**$6,350**

fig. 10.3

The pension money and the 401(k) will be managed in a time-segmented withdrawal plan, with about 70 percent of the funds in conservative or fixed investments. The balance of 30 percent will be invested into various stock portfolios. According to our time segmentation models, the 30 percent in stocks will not be needed for income for fifteen to twenty years, so the stock can grow and mature as the long-term investment that it is.

When Ben and Darla combine all their sources of income, they'll have enough inflation-adjusted income to meet their retirement needs. Within the time-segmented strategy, the investments need to be monitored and harvested as each segment reaches its goals and objectives.

Situation Two: Bruce and Katherine

Bruce, sixty-seven, and Katherine, sixty-five, both worked hard to ensure that their cabinet-making business was a success. However, they couldn't sell their business for as much as they hoped, and they ended up short of their goals for retirement-fund accumulation. Bruce and Katherine built a new house, and, as is often the case, the expenses involved in building the house exceeded their expectations, resulting in a $1,500-per-month mortgage payment. Further complicating their situation are Bruce's health problems, which do not allow him to work part-time as he'd originally planned to do during retirement. They need a monthly income of $4,600 to make ends meet (see figure 10.4).

Sources of Income	Total Monthly Income
Income Goal: $4,600	
Source of Income 1: Social Security	
The nice thing about owning a business is that there are a lot of write-offs, so a business owner can keep income low for tax purposes. The not-so-nice thing about owning a business is that because incomes are kept low, so are Social Security contributions. Bruce will only receive $1,100 per month during retirement, and Katherine will receive $560 per month. Even though they know they could wait to apply for their Social Security benefits and receive more, they really need the income from Social Security—now. $1,100 + $560=$1,660	$1,660
Source of Income 2: Pension Plan	
Because Bruce was self-employed, he does not have a pension plan. Katherine worked as a secretary at a university for a period of time and will be receiving $390 monthly. No lump sum payout is available.	$390
Source of Income 3: Employment	
Bruce was planning to work during retirement at the business he sold. However, because of health reasons, his doctors say that his dream of working during retirement will never be realized.	$0
Source of Income 4: Reverse Mortgage	
With the sale of the business and their old house, Bruce and Katherine managed to put a rather large lump sum on their newly built home. They have a loan of $250,000 on a house that has been appraised at $500,000. The interest rate is 6.42 percent, but the payment of $1,500 monthly is difficult. Bruce and Katherine decided to do a reverse mortgage. *In their case, the reverse mortgage will not give them a monthly income, but it will eliminate the monthly mortgage payment of $1,500.*	$1,500.00 mortgage payment eliminated

Source of Income 5: Investment Income	
An immediate annuity purchased with a lump sum of money prior to their retirement will provide $355 monthly for the life spans of both Bruce and Katherine. After selling their business and putting a $250,000 payment on a house, they were left with $250,000 to create an income stream. According to the 5 percent withdrawal rate, they can expect $1,041 monthly out of their investments. $355 (Immediate Annuity Income)+ $1,041 (Investment Income)= $1,396	$1,396
Total Monthly Income	$3,446

fig. 10.4

In Bruce and Katherine's case, the retirement income planner couldn't provide the $4,600 of monthly income originally desired, but the couple was able to lower their income need by $1,500 by wiping out their mortgage payment with a reverse mortgage. Now they only need $3,100 a month to make ends meet. Therefore, this plan leaves them $346 in excess of their desired monthly income goal. Had they not done a reverse mortgage, their only other option besides downsizing their house would have been to take a 12.25 percent withdrawal rate on their investment portfolio, which would have depleted their savings and investments in a few short years.

Situation Three: Jerry and Ann

Jerry, sixty-six, is a professor at a large university in the area. He has worked for the university for thirty years and has built a large pension, as well as a healthy 401(k) portfolio. Ann, sixty-five, has worked as a stay-at-home mom, and therefore hasn't built up any Social Security or pension benefits. They need $8,000 monthly to meet their retirement income goals (see fig. 10.5).

Sources of Income	Total Monthly Income
Income Goal: $8,000	
Source of Income 1: Social Security	
Jerry will receive $2,100, and Ann will receive 50 percent of that ($1,050) once she reaches her full retirement age of sixty-six in about a year. $2,100+1,050=$3,150	$3,150
Source of Income 2: Pension Plan	
The university has a pension plan, but does not allow lump-sum roll-overs. Jerry and Ann will only be allowed to receive a monthly income, and they must choose between the various survivor benefits available as part of the pension plan. Jerry is an insulin-dependent diabetic and is therefore uninsurable. Because he can't buy life insurance, they have no opportunities for pension maximization. They therefore decide on a survivor benefit that would maximize income to Ann given Jerry's shortened life-expectancy. The 100 percent joint and survivor option will provide $3,700 monthly for as long as Jerry or Ann lives.	$3,700
Source of Income 3: Employment	
Jerry and Ann wish to spend time during retirement doing humanitarian and missionary work, and do not have the desire or need to work during retirement.	$0
Source of Income 4: Reverse Mortgage	
Their home is paid off, and they do not plan on tapping that income source unless an unforeseen emergency occurs.	$0

Source of Income 5: Investment Income	
Jerry and Ann meet all but about $1,150 of their monthly income needs through Social Security and their pension. Therefore, they will only need to take a very reasonable 3 percent withdrawal rate from their savings and investment portfolios, which total $453,000. Most of that money is in a 401(k), but they have a "junk drawer" of small CDs and Roth IRAs that need to be integrated into an overall retirement income plan. Jerry and Ann are conservative investors, but they recognize the need to have some stocks in a retirement income portfolio in order to keep up with inflation. They invest 50 percent of their investment balance into a conservative bond mix in a brokerage account. They invest the other 50 percent of their money in a 100 percent stock sub-account in a variable annuity. They chose a guaranteed minimum withdrawal rider (GMWB), which guarantees that, at a minimum, the principal invested in the annuity will be returned to them over time, plus annual step-ups, even if the stock market plummets. Because of Jerry's diabetes, they also add a death benefit rider to their annuity. This will guarantee to Ann the highest annuity anniversary value or the account balance at Jerry's death, whichever is greater. They recognize that the GMWB guarantee and death benefit cost about 1.5 percent more than a mutual fund per year, but they feel the extra fee is worth the peace of mind. Jerry and Ann implement a time-segmented strategy to help achieve the monthly income they desire. Because they are only drawing 3 percent, their investment portfolio should grow, leaving an inheritance for their children and grandchildren.	$1,150
Total Monthly Income	**$8,000**

fig. 10.5

Jerry and Ann's lifetime of frugality has paid off. They have planned and saved well and look forward to a dependable stream of income that should last throughout their retirement.

Conclusion

All three couples' situations are unique, as is every retiree's situation. That is why a customized retirement income plan is so important to the new retiree. You need to establish an income goal, then work toward that goal through recognizing and maximizing the five sources of income. Know what you really want, and then make it happen through careful planning and investment discipline.

CHAPTER 12

CHOOSING THE
RIGHT ADVISOR

I've been known to fix my own cars, shampoo my own carpets, and do my own yard work, even though professionals in these respective areas can probably do these tasks better and more cost efficiently than I can. I guess you can blame it on my heritage; I've been told that I'm frugal and tightfisted like the Scottish, and independent and bullheaded like the Swiss.

Over the years, however, I've come to know my own limitations. I don't file my own taxes, raise my own beef, or perform surgical procedures on myself—all of these activities require expertise and resources I simply don't have. Likewise, if you think you can manage the retirement distribution phase of life all by yourself, you might need to recognize your own limitations.

Remember: it is much easier to accumulate a retirement than it is to properly distribute one. First, you must develop expertise in investment management, investment products, taxation, estate planning, Social Security planning, pension planning, mortgages, insurance, and withdrawal strategies, and keep up to date in these ever-changing topics. You would also have to purchase, learn to use, and update sophisticated planning software. Don't underestimate the overwhelming amount of knowledge needed to successfully construct a retirement income plan.

At the time of this writing, I have a quarter of a century of experience working with retirees and studying the issues surrounding retirement income planning. I have come to know my own limitations and have therefore surrounded myself with a competent, mature staff that is invaluable to the individual success of each client. I work with a large team of professionals such as attorneys, CPAs, insurance agents, bankers, mortgage brokers, mutual fund managers, and economists. As a team, we strive to produce state-of-the-art solutions for our mutual clients, and to provide the best possible opportunity for those clients to reach their respective financial goals. All of this knowledge and the development of a retirement income planning team would be nearly impossible for an individual to duplicate.

What Does an Investment Advisor Actually Do?

The investment advisor fulfills three critical functions:

First, he develops formal financial, estate, and retirement income plans with the client. These plans drive all of the financial decisions of the client and thus need to be goal-oriented, current, and reviewed at least annually. Changes to the plans should be implemented only when clients make major life changes or alter their goals significantly.

Second, the investment advisor comes to know the client and constructs an investment plan specific to their risk tolerance, time horizon, age, income needs, and so forth. He then selects from among the thousands of mutual funds, exchange-traded funds, variable annuities, unit-investment trusts, and myriad other investments to find the proper products in the proper quantities that best fit their situation. The product selection should be determined by the experience and longevity of the manager and the fee structures and tax burdens of the various products. He then monitors the properly diversified, low-correlated portfolio and occasionally adjusts it as needed.

Third, in addition to all an investment advisor must know and do, he must save retirees from their own destructive investment behavior. Whether it's keeping them from liquidating all of their stocks when the stock market is down 30 percent (which, on the average, happens once every five years) or trying to talk them out of buying that latest trendy stock that has already gone up 200 percent, the advisor's most important function is to provide an educated, experienced, and independent voice of reason. A well-constructed, goal-oriented retirement income plan will help the retiree have the discipline necessary to survive the volatile investment environment that they'll occasionally experience.

How Do Retirement Income Planners Get Paid?

Different types of financial advisors are compensated in various ways for managing investments. Typically, the cost of employing a financial professional will be somewhere between 1 to 1.5 percent of the annual value of the investment portfolios that are being managed. In his book *Simple Wealth, Inevitable Wealth*, Nick Murray asked some thought-provoking questions regarding the use of an advisor: "Will working with an advisor add more than 1 percent (or whatever) to your total lifetime return? Does it seem probable to you that the advisor's counsel will (a) increase your return by more than 1 percent per year, (b) save you more than 1 percent a year in mistakes he or she helps you not to make, (c) save you time, effort, and worry that is worth more than 1 percent a year to you, and/or (d) all of the above?"[4] I believe the answer to Mr. Murray's questions are obvious; the real question is not, Should I hire an advisor to help me construct a retirement

---

4. Nick Murray, *Simple Wealth, Inevitable Wealth*, 27.

income plan? but rather, How do I find the right financial advisor to help me with all the essential decisions and management issues of my retirement?

Before you start searching for a qualified retirement income planner, it's important that you understand how these individuals are compensated. Investment professionals are paid in one of two ways:

1. They receive a commission for selling an investment product such as stocks, bonds, mutual funds, and variable annuities. Commissioned investment professionals are called *registered representatives*, and sell their products through entities called broker dealers.

2. They receive compensation for investment management on an ongoing fee basis, typically in the form of a percentage of assets under management. A typical fee ranges from 1 percent to 1.5 percent of the annual account value. For example, a management fee of 1 percent for a million-dollar account would be ten thousand dollars annually. Investment professionals who collect a fee and are not affiliated with a broker dealer are referred to as *registered investment advisors* (RIAs).

Investment professionals don't have to decide to exclusively be registered representatives (commission-based) or registered investment advisors (fee-based). Many investment professionals are dually registered in order to provide the broadest access to products and services.

Besides registered representatives and registered investment advisors, individuals licensed to sell insurance can sell a very limited selection of retirement products, such as fixed annuities or immediate annuities. These products in and of themselves aren't enough to produce a viable retirement income plan.

The Qualified Retirement Income Planner

In chapter 2, I compared typical investment advisors and retirement income planners to lift operators and ski instructors. The lift operator (investment advisor) helps you get up the mountain (accumulate money for retirement). This advisor could be a 401(k) representative, a financial advisor, or perhaps the prospective retiree himself. As long as the skier (retiree) didn't make critical mistakes such as jumping off the ski lift (abandoning the funding of retirement accounts), everything usually works out well. Alternatively, the skilled ski instructor (the retirement income planner) is the professional who helps the skier get down the mountain safely (distribute retirement assets). Potential hazards are numerous on the ride down the mountain, and the experience of a professional is critical.

The point I want to make is that, just because the retiree has known and worked with the same investment advisor for years, that doesn't mean that investment advisor is knowledgeable and educated enough in retirement issues and retirement distribution methodologies to get the retiree safely through retirement. Retirement income planning is a specialty, and the financial futures of retirees and their families should be handled by an investment advisor who has developed competency in retirement income planning.

How to Find a Retirement Income Planner

The retiree-to-be should choose a retirement income planner much as they'd choose a doctor, attorney, CPA, or any other professional. The best way to find an advisor is to get a referral from another trusted professional who deals with financial issues, such as a CPA or an attorney. You might also consider a referral from a friend in circumstances similar to yours.

Ask the professional or trusted friend whom they would trust to manage their money during retirement. Once you've gathered some names, and before you ask the extensive questions listed below, perform a litmus test by asking your potential retirement income planner two simple questions: When should I take Social Security, and what is a healthy, sustainable withdrawal rate? If the investment advisor says you should take Social Security right away to get as much out of the system as possible or gives some other generic answer, they're not a retirement income planner. In addition, if they don't have a legitimate answer ready when asked about withdrawal rates, they're not a retirement income planner; investment advisors who specialize in retirement income planning know that a withdrawal rate beyond 5 percent can be risky. An investment advisor who doesn't give you the right answers to these questions may be good at accumulating but probably won't be helpful during your retirement's distribution phase.

Regulation of Investment Professionals

Registered Representatives

Registered representatives, or those who sell security products for a commission, must be registered with a brokerage firm (also known as a broker dealer). The Financial Industry Regulatory Authority (FINRA) is the private-sector regulator of the U.S. securities industry. All registered representatives must pass criminal, personal, and financial background checks, and be sponsored by a broker dealer. They must also pass at least one of several licensing examinations, and meet continuing education requirements. You should check a registered representative's background through FINRA's web site before you make a final decision to work with a specific advisor.

Registered Investment Advisors

Those who receive fees for managing money are called registered investment advisors and are regulated either by the states in which they live or by the Securities and Exchange Commission (SEC) depending on how much money they manage. See the resources page to find out how you can research SEC registered investment advisors.

Questions to Ask the Potential Investment Advisor

After performing that simple litmus test, set up an appointment and interview a couple of investment professionals who passed the test. At first, you may feel awkward asking an advisor to answer some of the following questions, but remember: it's important to establish trust with the person who will be handling your family's financial future. If during the initial interview, your potential investment advisor makes recommendations or tries to sell you a product without understanding your specific situation, then he's not doing his job. You need to get to know them and they need to get to know you before they can make suitable recommendations for your individual circumstances. There are too many good investment advisors out there to settle on one who doesn't do his homework prior to recommending investments. Find another advisor!

Here are some interview questions you should ask:

1. **What are your qualifications, background, and education?** Listen for experience and skills that could be used to create a retirement income plan. Beware of such red flags as being new to the business, working only part-time, or mostly working with young executives rather than retirees. Don't be overly impressed with titles such as wealth manager, senior specialist, account executive, financial advisor, or vice-president of investments. In reality, such titles are usually concocted purely for marketing purposes and do not indicate any special knowledge or ability. However, a couple of titles such as CFP (Certified Financial Planner) and ChFC (Chartered Financial Consultant) do require passing stringent tests and completing continuing education. To clarify, there is no governing body or professional designation for those who create "retirement income plans." These plans are typically put

together by investment professionals who have specialized in working with retirees throughout their careers.

2. **Tell me about your licenses and registrations and explain to me how you get paid.** You should be able to quickly find out if the person is a commission-based advisor (registered representative), a fee-based advisor (registered investment advisor), or both. Registered representatives get a commission from each product they sell, and those commissions vary product to product. Registered investment advisors should be able to produce an outline of their fee schedules, as part of a document called a Form ADV. I believe there is a place for both commission-based and fee-based planners, so you should not rule someone out solely on this basis. Asking the question will simply give you more insight into how the advisor operates.

3. **Have you been disciplined for any unlawful or unethical actions in your professional career?** Although you need to ask this question during the interview, you should verify it beforehand online (see additional resources page). Don't settle for an advisor with complaints or an extensive history of moving from firm to firm.

4. **What should I expect you to do for me?** A good advisor will say things such as "evaluate risk tolerance," "establish time horizons," "select suitable investments," "rebalance portfolios," and "help you formulate and stick to a retirement income plan." Many advisors provide an investment policy statement (IPS) detailing individualized investment strategies that the advisor will follow in addition to written financial plans. Some advisors may have elaborate written financial plans, but those plans aren't worth much if they don't use realistic assumptions as far as inflation rate, rates of return, etc.

5. **What does your staff do? How many clients do you serve?** These questions help the retiree know if the advisor tries to cut corners and do it all on his own, or if he has a well-staffed organization that can take care of the client when the advisor is away. It would be very difficult for an advisor to truly plan and implement retirement income properly without staff. Even if he has a good staff, if the advisor serves hundreds of clients he will not have the time to specialize in anything, let alone the often complicated and time-consuming tasks of retirement income planning.

6. **How would we develop a retirement plan if I became a client?** Listen for clues to see if the investment advisor would really get to know your situation, not just your investments. Family, housing, health, lifestyle, and any other concerns you might have must be discussed.

7. **How would you describe your ideal client?** Ideally, the advisor would describe *you*. If they describe a high-flying, risk-taking young executive, you should probably look elsewhere. A follow-up question is: Do you have account minimums? You don't want to be the largest account the advisor takes care of, because they may not have the experience or expertise to handle a larger account. You don't want to be the smallest account the advisor has, either, because then you won't get the attention you deserve.

8. **How often will we communicate, and in what form?** Listen to the investment advisor's answer and then voice your expectations. Remember, the investment advisor works for you. Some retirees like quarterly face-to-face reviews, while some only want annual reviews. Accessibility is the key: the investment advisor should be there when you feel you need him. The advisor should make ongoing efforts through web sites, newsletters, e-mails, client events, workshops, and more to keep you informed.

9. **How would you potentially invest my money?** When looking for a professional to provide a retirement income plan, avoid a "market timer," a "stock picker," or a promiser of 30 percent returns. You want solid market returns and, most importantly, a plan that can be implemented to provide inflation-adjusted income. I don't know anybody who can time the market, so be wary of those who try to convince you that they can. Also, listen to see if the investment advisor moves in and out of different investments often. This usually produces a lot of unnecessary trading costs and has not shown to increase investment results.

10. **Do you have a working relationship with other professionals? Who? How closely do you work with them?** A retirement income planner should be the quarterback of a retirement income team and should be able to coordinate all activities involving the client. However, a quarterback is not a whole team, and your planner needs to work closely with the other members of the team, including CPAs, attorneys, and so on. Retirement income planners should recognize their own limitations. They're not trained or qualified to provide technical tax planning or legal advice. Maximizing all the sources of retirement income does not happen in a vacuum; long-term success entails careful consultation with tax, legal, and other professionals.

After you choose an investment advisor to create and implement your retirement income plan, you'll need to ask questions and stay intimately involved in the planning process. After all, your future lifestyle (and the lifestyle of your loved ones) depends on the success of your plan.

Ideally, the retirement income planner will become part of your inner circle. The planner should come to know your dreams, goals, and concerns, and should be there during the life-changing events of retirement, such as sickness or the death of a spouse. A good retirement income planner will be there during good and bad economic times, developing your trust and providing you with the confidence and discipline necessary to stick with a well-thought-out plan that will maximize your income for a long and financially successful retirement.

CONCLUSION

The decisions you make at retirement and your subsequent management of investments are critical. Simply put, a properly designed and implemented retirement income plan can help you realize your dream of a financially secure retirement. Lack of planning could turn even the best-funded retirement into a nightmare.

As the baby boomers retire, it is my hope that each retiree be able to concentrate on those things that are truly meaningful to them—things besides money. This hope will only be accomplished through careful planning, discipline, and retirees taking personal responsibility for managing their retirement.

The financial challenges facing today's retirees are many, but likewise, the opportunities are unmatched in history. May each of you find success and fulfillment in whatever retirement dream you pursue.

ADDITIONAL RESOURCES

Peterson Financial Website

- http://www.petersonfinancial.net

Peterson Financial Income for Life® Website and Movie

- http://www.speterson.retirementtime.com

Budgeting Web Sites

- http://www.quicken.intuit.com
- http://www.personalbudgeting.com
- http://www.fidelity.com (Keyword "Full View")

Pension Benefit Guaranty Corporation

- http://www.pbgc.gov

Full-Time RVing

- http://www.goodsamclub.com/
- http://fulltimeRVer.com/

Background Checks on Financial Advisors

- www.finra.org (Registered Representatives/commissioned-based)
- www.adviserinfo.sec.gov (Registered Investment Advisors/ fee-based)

Social Security Online

- www.ssa.gov

GLOSSARY

401(k): A defined contribution plan offered by an employer to employees, which allows employees to set aside tax-deferred income for retirement purposes. In some cases employers will match their contribution. See also *Defined Contribution Plan*.

American Association of Retired Persons (AARP): an association to promote the welfare of senior citizens.

Actuarial Reduction: The reduction of a Social Security benefit when taken before full retirement age. The reduction is permanent and is designed to provide, on the average, the same value of total lifetime benefits as would have been payable if the benefits had started at full retirement age.

Asset Allocation: The process of dividing investments among different kinds of assets, such as stocks, bonds, real estate and cash, to optimize risk-reward tradeoffs based on an individual's or institution's specific situation and goals.

Baby Boomer: A person born between 1946 and 1964.

Bear Market: A market condition in which the prices of securities are falling or are expected to fall. Although figures can vary, a downturn of 15-20 percent or more in multiple indexes (Dow or S&P 500) is considered an entry into a bear market.

Break-Even Age: The age at which a Social Security recipient would receive more benefits by waiting to take their benefit at a later age. See chapter 4 for a detailed analysis.

Bull Market: A financial market of a certain group of securities in which prices are rising or are expected to rise. The term "bull market" is most often used in respect to the stock market, but really can be applied to anything that is traded, such as bonds, currencies, commodities, etc.

Certificate of Deposit (CD): A short- or medium-term, FDIC-insured debt instrument offered by banks. CDs offer higher rates of return than most comparable investments, in exchange for tying up invested money for the duration of the certificate's maturity. CDs are low-risk, low-return investments.

Certified Public Accountant (CPA): The title of qualified accountants in the United States who have passed the Uniform Certified Public Accountant Examination and have met additional state education and experience requirements.

Cost of Living Adjustment (COLA): An annual adjustment in Social Security to offset a change (usually a loss) in purchasing power, as measured by the Consumer Price Index.

Consumer Price Index (CPI): An indicator of inflation that measures the change in the cost of products and services, including housing, electricity, food, and transportation. The CPI is published monthly and is also known as the cost-of-living index.

Contract Value: The actual value of an annuity contract.

Correlation: A concept used to measure diversification in a portfolio. Assets which tend to move in opposition to each other are negatively correlated. Low correlated assets tend to move independently of each other. A range of negatively correlated and low correlated assets in a portfolio is designed to help reduce losses in all sectors of a portfolio at the same time.

Death Benefit Guarantee: The payment made to a beneficiary after the owner of an annuity or policy dies. It is guaranteed to be a certain percentage added to the original principle or the highest value, whichever is higher.

Defined Benefit Plan: A company retirement plan, such as a pension plan, in which a retired employee receives a specific monthly income based on salary history and years of service, and in which the employer bears the investment risk.

Defined Contribution Plan: A company retirement plan, such as a 401(k) plan, in which the employee elects to defer some amount of his salary into the plan and bears the investment risk.

Diversification: A strategy to reduce risk in a portfolio by combining a variety of investments, such as stocks, bonds, and real estate, which are unlikely to all move simultaneously in the same direction. Therefore, the benefits of diversification are incresed if the securities in the portfolio are not highly correlated.

Divorced Spouse Benefit: A Social Security provision that allows a divorced spouse to collect half of the value of an ex-spouse's Social Security benefit, if greater than his or her own.

Earnings Test: A Social Security test that effectively defers benefits for people are under full retirement age and whose earnings are above a given threshold. When a worker who was subject to the earnings test reaches full retirement age, the earnings test no longer applies and monthly benefits are increased to replace those denied by the earnings test.

Employee Retirement Income Security Act of 1974 (ERISA): A federal law established legal guidelines for private pension plan administration and investment practices.

Equities: Ownership interest in a corporation in the form of common stock or preferred stock.

Estate Plan: Written document setting out an estate owner's instructions for disposition and administration of his or her property at his or her death, incapacity, or total disability.

Exchange Traded Funds (ETF): A security that tracks an index, a commodity, or a basket of assets much as an index fund does, but which trades like a stock on an exchange. It thus experiences price changes throughout the day as it is bought and sold.

Federal Deposit Insurance Corporation (FDIC): A federal agency that insures deposits in member banks and thrifts up to $100,000 in regular years. With the recent recession, the insured amount has been raised to $250,000 until December 31, 2013.

Financial Industrial Regulatory Authority (FINRA): A self-regulatory organization responsible for the operation and regulation of the Nasdaq stock market and over-the-counter markets. FINRA investigates complaints against member firms and tries to ensure that all of its members adhere to both its own standards and those laid out by the Securities and Exchange Commission.

Fixed Annuity: An investment vehicle offered by an insurance company that guarantees a stream of fixed payments over the life of the annuity. The insurer, not the insured, takes on the investment risk.

Form ADV: A required submission by a registered investment advisor (RIA) to the Securities and Exchange Commission (SEC) or the state in which the RIA resides that specifies the investment style, assets under management (AUM), and key officers of the firm.

Full Retirement Age (FRA): The age, set forth either by a retirement plan or by Social Security, at which employees receive full benefits upon retirement. Retiring before FRA may result in a reduction in benefits. Most corporate plans specify sixty-five as the normal retirement age. Social Security has a sliding retirement age. See fig. 4.1 for specifics.

Guaranteed Minimum Withdrawal Benefit (GMWB): An optional rider that protects retirement annuities against downside market risk by guaranteeing the entire initial investment. The owner of the annuity has the right to withdraw a certain percentage of his or her entire investment each year until the initial investment amount has been recouped.

Harvesting Strategy: A strategy used in time segmented distribution plan to ensure that gains are locked in. Once investments have reached their goals, they are liquidated and then put into safer investments until they are scheduled for use as income. Although this limits growth in excess of the goal amount, it helps reduce risk in the harvested segment of a retirement portfolio.

Home Equity Conversion Mortgage (HECM): The only type of reverse mortgage insured by the federal government; an arrangement in which a homeowner borrows against the equity in his or her home and receives regular monthly tax-free payments from the lender. The amount to be repaid can never exceed the amount borrowed with an HECM.

Department of Housing and Urban Development (HUD): A federal agency that encourages housing development.

Immediate Annuity: An annuity in which payments to the annuitant or beneficiary start at once upon establishment of the annuity plan. Such annuities are almost always purchased with a single (lump sum) payment.

Inflation: Sustained, rapid increase in the general levels of prices, as measured by a broad index number (such as the Consumer Price Index) over months or years, and mirrored in the correspondingly decreasing purchasing power of the currency.

IRA: Tax-deferred retirement plans that can be started by anyone who earns employment income. Individuals who earn less than a certain amount (or who do not participate in their employer's retirement plan) can generally deduct part or all of their contributions to such plans from their taxable income. Money in an IRA is taxed only when it is withdrawn. See also *Roth IRA*.

Liquid Asset: Cash, or any asset that is easily and quickly convertible into cash.

Liquidity: The degree to which an asset or security can be bought or sold in the market without affecting the asset's price. Liquid assets are characterized by a high level of trading activity.

Longevity risk: The risk that an individual's retirement savings might run out, due to increased life expectancy.

Market Correction: A reversal of the prevailing price trends for securities. The term is most often used to describe a decline after a period of rising prices. A correction is often considered beneficial for the long-term health of the market, in that it restores prices that have risen too quickly to more realistic levels.

Medicare: A federal program that pays for certain health care expenses for people aged sixty-five or older. Enrolled individuals must pay deductibles and co-payments, but many of their medical costs are covered by the program. Medicare is divided into three parts: Part A covers hospitals' bills, Part B covers doctors' bills, and Part C provides different health care plans from which to choose.

Medigap: Various supplementary private health insurance plans available to Medicare recipients that cover medical expenses excluded from or only partially covered by Medicare.

Mutual Fund: A type of professionally managed collective investment plan that pools money from many investors and places it in a combination of stocks, bonds, short-term money market instruments, or other securities. A fund manager trades the pooled money on a regular basis. The net proceeds or losses are then typically distributed to the investors annually.

Old Age, Survivors, and Disability Insurance (OASDI): The official name for Social Security.

Pension Benefit Guaranty Corporation (PBGC): A federal corporation established in 1974 under ERISA, which insures the vested benefits of pension plan participants. PBGC also sets a maximum guaranteed benefit which changes yearly; as of 2009 the maximum benefit for someone who retires at age sixty-five was $4,500 a month.

Pension: Post-retirement benefits and compensation that certain employers award to their employees. Pensions are less common today, and were originally designed to reward long-term loyalty to a company. See also *Defined Benefit Plan*

Poor Laws: An outdated law or system of laws providing for public relief and support of the poor; originated in England under Tudor rule.

Protected Balance: The guaranteed amount of money that the owner of an annuity can withdraw during his lifetime. Initially, the protected balance is the principal invested into the annuity; thereafter, this guaranteed balance may be increased through "step-ups."

Recareering: Changing careers late in working life or after retirement. Recareering is not just a job change within an industry or company, but rather a move to a completely different career path.

Registered Representative (RR): An individual who is licensed to sell securities and has the legal power of an agent, having passed the Series 7 and Series 63 examinations. Usually registered representatives work for brokerages licensed by the SEC, NYSE, and NASD.

Registered Investment Advisor (RIA): Registered Investment Advisor (RIA): A company that makes investment recommendations or conducts securities analysis in return for a fee, whether through direct management of client assets or via written publications.

Retirement Income Plan: A financial plan tailored to the specific needs of the retiree, which takes into account longevity and inflation and seeks to provide the necessary income at the lowest possible risk.

Reverse Mortgage: An arrangement in which homeowners borrow against the equity in their homes and receive regular monthly tax-free payments from the lender. Only principle residences who have paid off a certain percentage of their mortgages qualify for these loans.

Risk Tolerance: An investor's ability to handle declines in the value of his portfolio.

Roth IRA: A new type of IRA, established in the Taxpayer Relief Act of 1997, which allows retirement savings to grow tax-free. Taxes are paid on contributions to the Roth IRA, but withdrawals are not taxed. Contributions to the Roth IRA are invested in mutual funds, stocks, or other securities. The maximum amount that an individual is allowed to contribute is dependent upon their income, age, and tax filing status.

Securities and Exchange Commission: The primary federal regulatory agency for the securities industry, whose responsibility is to promote full disclosure and to protect investors against fraudulent and manipulative practices in the securities markets.

Senior Citizens' Freedom to Work Act of 2000: Provision in the Social Security Legislative Bulletin 106-20 that allows senior citizens to apply for Social Security but suspend their benefits while they continue working. This allows a nonworking spouse to collect a spousal benefit while the worker accrues delayed credits.

Social Security: A comprehensive federal program that provides workers and their dependents with retirement income, disability income, and other payments. The Social Security tax is used to pay for the program.

Spousal Benefit: A provision of Social Security that allows spouses to collect one half (50 percent) of their spouse's Social Security benefit if it is larger than their own.

Survivor Benefit: A provision of Social Security that provides surviving spouses with the higher of two benefits—either their own benefit or their deceased spouse's benefit.

Time Horizon: The length of time a sum of money is expected to be invested.

Time Segmented Distribution Plan: An income distribution plan that provides a balanced combination of conservative, moderate, and aggressive investments to pursue long-term retirement goals. Investments are divided into segments that are allowed to grow for a certain period of time before being harvested for income. Each segment is set up to provide income for a certain number of years. Segments with more risk are allocated less money, but the riskier segments provide more growth opportunity and are therefore designated for longer-term, fifteen- to twenty-year periods.

Timing the Market: Timing investment activities, such as buying and selling, in the belief that future market directions can be predicted and exploited.

Unit Investment Trusts (UIT): An unmanaged trust sold by a SEC-registered investment company. The investment company purchases fixed, unmanaged portfolios of securities and then sells shares in these trusts to investors. The major difference between a unit investment trust and a mutual fund is that some mutual funds are actively managed, while a unit investment trust is not actively managed after its creation.

Variable Annuity: A life insurance annuity contract which provides future payments to the annuity holder, usually at retirement. The size of the payments depends on the performance of the portfolio's securities.

Volatility: A measure of the amount and frequency with which a security fluctuates up or down. Commonly, the higher the volatility, the riskier the security.

Withdrawal Rate: The annual percentage of income withdrawn from a portfolio. In a retirement portfolio, 4 percent to 5 percent is considered the most reasonable and sustainable withdrawal rate.

BIBLIOGRAPHY

AARP Foundation. *Reverse Mortgage Loans: Borrowing Against your Home.* Booklet, 2008. http://assets.aarp.org/www.aarp.org_/articles/money/financial_pdfs/hmm_hires_nocrops.pdf.

Anenson, T. Leigh and Karen Eilers Lahey. "The Crisis in Corporate America: Private Pension Liability and Proposals for Reform." *Journal of Labor and Employment Law* 9, no. 3 (2007): 495–531.

AXA Group. *Social Security.* Report prepared by Advanced Market Division, 2008.

Beland, Daniel. *Social Security: History and Politics from the New Deal to the Privatization Debate.* Kansas: University Press of Kansas, 2007.

Christensen, Karen. "Thought Leader Interview: William Sharpe." *The Rotman Magazine* (Spring 2008): 10–13.

Congressional Budget Office. *Updated Long-Term Projections for Social Security: Potential Range of Scheduled Social Security Outlays and Revenues*, 2008.

Dalbar Institute. *Quantitative Analysis of Investor Behavior: What Investors Really Do…and How to Counteract It.* Extract from the report *QAIB 2008*. Advisor ed., 2008. http://www.scribd.com/doc/13096471/DALBAR-QAIB-2008.

DeBaca, Suzanna. "Why Work with a Financial Advisor." *Expert Business Source,* http://www.expertbusinesssource.com/article/CA6417746.html.

Delong, David. "Living Longer, Working Longer: The Changing Landscape of the Aging Workforce." *MetLife Mature Market Institute*. Brochure, 2006.

Ellis, Charles D. *Winning the Loser's Game: Timeless Strategies for Successful Investing*. New York: McGraw-Hill, 2002.

Elsasser, Joe, CFP and Dan Trumblee. "Better Buckets: Introducing the Sequent Income Model." *Senior Market Sales*. White paper, 2009.

Employee Benefit Research Institute. *EBRI General Benefits Research: Findings 2003*. http://www.ebri.org/media/findings/.

Fisher Investments. *The Eight Biggest Mistakes Investors Make and How to Avoid Them.* http://www.fi.com/fisher-investments-resources/eight-biggest-mistakes.aspx.

Floyd, Elaine, CFP. "Calculating the Financial Impact of Working Longer." *Horsesmouth,* 2009. http://www.horsesmouth.com/hm.asp?mode=&Flag=x&r=0.7714807.

———. "When to Apply for Social Security Benefits." *Horsesmouth*, 2008. http://www.horsesmouth.com/hm.asp?mode=&Flag= x&r=0.7714807.

———. *The Financial Advisors Guide to Savvy Social Security Planning for Boomers: A Client Education Program.* New York: Horsesmouth, 2008.

Franklin Templeton Investments. *RetireMetrics: Build a Better Retirement.* Brochure, 2009.

Gandel, Cathie. "Making Your House Work for You." *AARP Bulletin Today.* January, 2008. http://bulletin.aarp.org/your-money/personalfinance/articles/making_your_house.html.

Green, James J. "Solutions for the New Retirement Reality." *Investment Advisor*, 2009. http://www.investmentadvisor .com/Issues/2009/December-2009/Pages/Solutions-for-the -New-Retirement-Reality.aspx.

Hamilton, Martha M. "Working Longer—The Best Way to Afford Retirement." *AARP Bulletin Today.* January 15, 2009. http://bulletin.aarp.org/yourmoney/retirement/articles /working_longer_the_best_way_to_afford_retirement .comments.0.html.

Hartford Leaders Outlook. *Annuities Designed to Help Grow and Protect YourRetirement Income.* Advisors Brochure, September 2008.

Hofschire, Dirk, CFA. "How Will the Bear Market End? Historical Patterns of Stock Market Reversals." *Fidelity*, March 27, 2009. http://publications.fidelity.com/investorsWeekly/application /loadArticle?pagename=IW090327marebear.

Holzer, Bambi. *Set for Life: Financial Peace for People over Fifty.* 1st ed. Hoboken, NJ: Wiley, 2000.

Ibbotson, Roger G. and Rex A. Sinquefield. *SBBI 2007 Yearbook: Market Results for 1926–2007: Stocks, Bonds, Bills, and Inflation (SBBI) Yearbook.* Classic ed. Chicago: Ibbotson Associates, 2007.

———. *SBBI 2008 Yearbook: Market Results for 1926–2008: Stocks, Bonds, Bills, and Inflation (SBBI) Yearbook.* Classic ed. Chicago: Ibbotson Associates, 2008.

———. *SBBI 2009 Yearbook: Market Results for 1926-2009: Stocks, Bonds, Bills, and Inflation (SBBI) Yearbook.* Classic ed. Chicago: Ibbotson Associates, 2009.

ING Financial & Investment. *Pension Maximization: A Strategy Using Life Insurance*, Advisors Brochure, 2004.

Jason, Julie. *The AARP Retirement Survival Guide: How to Make Smart Financial Decisions in Good Times and Bad.* New York: Sterling, 2009.

John Hancock. *Venture Variable Annuities: Variable Annuity Overview.* Advisors Brochure, 2009.

Johnson, Richard, Janette Kawachi, and Eric Lewis. "Older Workers on the Move: Recareering in Later Life." *The Urban Institute*, 2009. http://www.urban.org/url.cfm?ID=1001272.

J.P. Morgan Asset Management. "Asset Class: Corporate DB Plans and Endowments." *Market Insight Series.* Advisors Market Charts Kit, 2008.

Lubinski, Philip, Paul Lofties, and Zachary Parker. "Capturing the Income Distribution Opportunity." *Securities America.* White paper, 2007.

Morningstar. "Potential Shortfall: The Risk of High Withdrawal Rates," Advisors Market Charts Kit, 2009.

Morningstar. "Probability of Meeting Income Needs," Advisors Market Charts Kit, 2009.

Morningstar. "Reduction of Risk Over Time: Range of Returns 1926-2008," Advisors Market Charts Kit, 2009.

Morningstar. "The Cost of Market Timing: Risk of Missing the Best Days in the Market 1989-2008," Advisors Market Charts Kit, 2009.

Munnell, Alicia, Alex Golub-Sassm, and Nadia Karamcheva. "Strange but True: Claim Social Security Now, Claim More Later." *Issues in Brief series no. 9-9.* Boston: Center for Retirement Research at Boston College, April 2009. http://crr .bc.edu/images/stories/Briefs/ib_9-9.pdf.

Murray, Nick. *Behavioral Investment Counseling.* Southold, NY: Nick Murray Company, 2008.

———. *Simple Wealth, Inevitable Wealth.* Southold, NY: Nick Murray Company, 1999.

NewRetirement. *Advantages and Disadvantages of a Reverse Mortgage.* http://www.newretirement.com/services/Reverse_ Mortgage_Advantages_Disadvantages.aspx.

———. *Retirement Jobs: Working in Retirement.* http://www
.newretirement.com/services/working_in_retirement.aspx.

———. *Social Security Benefits Optimization: Social Security Info for Maximizing Your Social Security Benefits.* http://www
.newretirement.com/services/Social-Security-Benefits.aspx.

———. *What are the Best Jobs for Retirees? Retirement Careers and Where to Find Them.* http://www.newretirement.com
/Services/Working_In_Retirement_Best_Jobs.aspx.

———. *Working in "Retirement."* http://www.newretirement.com/
Services/Working_In_Retirement.aspx.

Pension Benefit Guaranty Corporation. *A Predictable, Secure Pension for Life: Defined Benefit Pensions,* January 2000. http://www
.pbgc.gov/docs/a_predictable_secure_pension_for_life.pdf.

Peterson, Scott M., ChFC. "The Informed Investor: Making Smart Investing Decisions in Today's Volatile Market." *Peterson Financial and Retirement Services,* 2003. http://www
.petersonwealthadvisors.net/Informed_Investor_peterson.
pdf.

Prudential. *The Arithmetic of Loss: The Reality of Market Declines,* Advisors Brochure, 2008.

Reno, Virginia and Joni Lavery. "Can We Afford Social Security When Baby Boomers Retire?" *National Academy of Social Insurance.* Social Security Brief No. 22, May 2006. http://
www.nasi.org/usr_doc/SS_Brief_022.pdf.

Smedley Financial Services, Inc. *SFS Proactive and Tax-Efficient Portfolios,* Advisors Brochure, 2009. http://www.advisorsquare

.com/new/smedleyfinancialservices/SFS%20Proactive%20P
ortfolios%20Client%20Use.pdf.

———. *Time-Segmented Investing Made Simple with New SFS Portfolios*, Advisors Brochure, 2009.

Social Security Administration. *Facts and Figures About Social Security.* Publication No. 13-11785, 2009. http://www.ssa.gov/policy /docs/chartbooks/fast_facts/2009/fast_facts09.pdf.

———. *Full Retirement Age.* http://www.socialsecurity.gov/retire2/ retirechart.htm.

———. *Historical Background and Development of Social Security.* http://www.ssa.gov/history/briefhistory3.

———. *Life Expectancy for Social Security.* http://www.ssa.gov /history/lifeexpect.

Society of Actuaries. *RP-2000 Mortality Tables*, 2000. http://www .soa.org/files/pdf/rp00_mortalitytables.pdf.

Swedroe, Larry. "The Smartest Things Ever Said about Market Timing." *CBS Money Watch.* Dec 25, 2009. http:// moneywatch.bnet.com/investing/blog/wise-investing/the-smartest-things-ever-said-about-market-timing/1089/.

Transamerica. *A Retirement Income Repair Strategy.* Annuity Guarantee Statement, 2009.

———. *Retirement Income Choice.* Advisors Brochure, 2008.

Trattner, William. *From Poor Law to Welfare State: A History of Social Welfare in America.* 6th ed. New York: The Free Press, 1999.

U.S. Bureau of Labor Statistics. *CPI-W, 1967-2008.* http://data
.bls.gov/PDQ/servlet/SurveyOutputServlet.

————. *CIP Detailed Report: Data for June 2009.* Report prepared
by Malik Crawford and Sanjeev Katz, June 2009.

U.S. Census Bureau. *Oldest Baby Booms Turn 60!* Facts for Features
Series no. CB06-FFSE.01-2, 2006. http://www.census.gov
/Press-Release/www/2006/cb06ffse01-2.pdf.

U.S. Congress. House. Social Security Board of Trustees. *The 2009
Annual Report of the Board of Trustees of the Federal Old-Age
and Survivors Insurance and Federal Disability Insurance Trust
Funds.* 111th Cong., 1st sess., 2009. H. Doc. 111-41.

————. *The 2003 Annual Report of the Board of Trustees of the Federal Old-Age and Survivors Insurance and Disability Insurance
Trust Funds.* 108th Cong., 1st sess., 2003. H. Doc. 108-49.

Wealth 2K. *The Income for Life Model: Concept Overview,* 2009.
http://www.incomeforlifemodel.com/PDF/IFLM_FINRA
/C_IFLM_CONCEPTOVERVIEW_2_DEMO.pdf.

Wells Fargo Home Mortgage. *Your Reverse Mortgage Guide.* Booklet, 2008.